POETRY AND POLITICS UNDER THE STUARTS

THE CLARK LECTURES
1958

POETRY AND POLITICS UNDER THE STUARTS

BY

C. V. WEDGWOOD

CAMBRIDGE
At the University Press
1961

PUBLISHED BY
THE SYNDICS OF THE CAMBRIDGE UNIVERSITY PRESS

Bentley House, 200 Euston Road, London, N.W. 1
American Branch: 32 East 57th Street, New York 22, N.Y.

©

CAMBRIDGE UNIVERSITY PRESS
1960

First Printed 1960
Reprinted 1961

Printed in Great Britain at the University Press, Cambridge
(Brooke Crutchley, University Printer)

PREFACE

This book is the text of the Clark Lectures given at Cambridge in the Lent Term of 1958. I should like to thank once again the Master and Fellows of Trinity College for their invitation to deliver these lectures and for the opportunity they thus so generously afforded me of developing a subject which I find deeply interesting. I should also like to thank the audience whose ready response to seventeenth-century wit made my task so pleasant.

The difference between the written and the spoken word is considerable. Although I have altered the text where the phrasing seemed altogether too colloquial to set down in print, I have on the whole left the lectures very much as I delivered them. Those who meet them for the first time in this form will, I hope, remember that what they are reading was written in the first place to be spoken, and that what runs easily in speech may sometimes hang slack in print, just as what reads smoothly in print may sometimes sound too contrived for easy speech.

The spelling of the numerous extracts from seventeenth-century writers is not consistent. I have given the original spelling and punctuation where I thought it added anything to the character of the ballad or poem. Where it did not do so, or where the peculiarities of the original text tended to obscure meaning, I have modernised for the sake of clarity.

C. V. W.

LONDON
June 1959

CONTENTS

I

COURT AND COUNTRY

The seventeenth century is one of the great ages of English history, a century of frequent tempests and deceptive calms, of tumultuous intellectual activity, of moral and physical conflict, of national expansion and social change. It is one of the great ages of politics, in thought, and in action, fruitful in ideas and experiments. It was inevitably a time of unrest and crisis, bringing forth civil war in England, Scotland and Ireland. The clash of interests between the nations of the British Isles, the differences between their social customs and the conflicts between their religious ideas confronted the Stuart kings with a greater complexity of problems than any of their predecessors had been called upon to face. In the traditional and simplified abbreviation of our national history the sovereigns of this dynasty come in for more criticism than they deserve for not solving problems which few rulers would have found comprehensible and none would have found easy.

The ferment of political activity, the quarrels over methods of government and religious dogma, the animosities which separated and the shifting alliances which united the peoples, their fears, hopes, ideals and misunderstandings were reflected in the varied literature of an immensely productive epoch. The century of Ben Jonson, Donne, Milton, Marvell and Dryden was rich in major talents, but it abounded also in minor talents. Writers of popular ballads were unceasingly prolific; in response to a new demand the press was born—a noisy, precocious infant; political satire developed from clumsy adolescence to ferocious maturity.

At the beginning of the Civil War the Royalist John Cleveland called up his fighting muse:

> Come keen iambics with your badgers feet
> And badger-like bite till your teeth do meet.

The angry promise of Cleveland's satirical verse, the most bitter that the Civil War produced, was fulfilled in a later generation when Dryden's keen-toothed iambics left scars on many a Whig reputation.

The century is remarkable for the ever increasing use of poetry (or verse to give it no higher name) in religious, social, and political controversy. Paradoxically, with this intensive use of verse as a weapon of attack in politics, the poetry of exaggerated and obsequious compliment, the courtly flattery of the men in power, reached its highest exaggeration. Its gracious elegance is in strange contrast to the vindictive ill-manners of political satire.

This region of political verse—the poetry directly inspired by public events and public figures—is less explored than other regions of our well-mapped literature. Apart from satire, which has its recognised place, poetry arising out of political events is not much considered by students of literature—for reasons which are evident. Even the most rigid believers in 'engaged' literature will allow that poetry directly inspired by passing events derives much of its vitality from emotions which, however violent at the time, are usually ephemeral; it therefore rarely rises to very great heights. A poem concerned with the temporary and the topical, however wittily ingenious it may be, however tense with the moment's passion, is never so strong a candidate for immortality as one inspired by a perennial theme.

Richard Lovelace and Lucasta are dust, but lines like:

> If to be absent were to be
> Away from thee

live partly by the magical rightness of their sound—that breathless run of short vowels followed by the yearning emphasis of the two long vowels—*away* from *thee*—but also because the theme of love and absence is common to all generations. It is a different matter with his 'Sonnet to General Goring after the Pacification at Berwick' in June 1639.[1] Even if it were a better poem than it is, it would have to surmount the drawback of a theme which is no longer of interest to anyone except the historian of the period, who may make a note of it in his card index under 'Goring, George, reputation of'.

Only the greatest poets are exempt from this rule. The political quarrel which gave rise to Dryden's *Absalom and Achitophel* is remote from us but the poem survives with its vitality only slightly impaired. It can be said with reasonable certainty that a reader of perception, with no knowledge at all of the circumstances and the protagonists, would still be captivated by the virtuosity of the writing, the felicitous use of adjectives, the sharpness of the characterisation, and the smooth subtlety of the sound. In much the same way, before the work of a great painter we are content to accept the title 'Portrait of an Unknown Man', and ask to know no more about him than what the painter has set down. But when we are looking at a lesser work of art some knowledge of the sitter or the subject does legitimately add to our appreciation of the picture, and ignorance of it may greatly reduce our pleasure.

In political verse generally speaking, understanding of the subject is important, and the merits of the poem fade as the content grows out of date and becomes incomprehensible or even antipathetic. Since it is no longer the fashion to 'make milch the burning eyes of heaven' whenever a prince dies, we are rarely touched by the floods of poetic brine that were shed on royal biers throughout the seventeenth

4

century. Rhetoric rings hollow; flowery compliments wilt, and the sharp edge of wit is blunted when half a page of footnotes is necessary to explain the meaning of the topical allusions.

This much may be safely argued without proceeding too far into that dangerous controversy on the relative importance of meaning and manner in poetry. But if political subject-matter is usually ephemeral, and if the highest in poetic achievement is rarely to be found associated with it, there is still in this region of uncertain frontiers, which lies midway between the departments of history and literature, much of incidental interest and some buried, or partly buried treasure.

It has been my fate and fortune in studying over the years the history of the seventeenth century to have read a great deal of political verse, and in so doing to have come across, sometimes in obvious, and sometimes in unexpected places, much that attracted by its charm or pleased by its ingenuity, and some little known fragments of real poetry. The student of history who is looking for facts and evidence, for sidelights on public opinion or straws in the political wind, necessarily approaches the material with a different eye from the student of literature proper. I cannot therefore hope to deal with the subtler questions of literary analysis. My net was cast very wide and took in the best and the worst, the elegant, learned and accomplished and the wholly unsophisticated. Ben Jonson and Milton treated of political themes; but so, not infrequently, did that fertile scribbler of jog-trot doggerel John Taylor the Water-poet; so did George Wither, among whose enormous output of mediocre scribbling there are (as well as the few lyrics made familiar by discriminating anthologists) several unusually vivid political poems, both satirical and heroic. There were also ballad-makers of no literary pretentions, but popular in their own day, and an invading horde of amateur scribblers who multiplied exceedingly throughout the century to the great annoyance of the professionals.

> This is the rhyming age, no wonder now
> To hear Thalia whistling at the plough.
> All traffic with the Muses; 'tis well known
> The sculler's boat can touch at Helicon....

sneered one university wit; and Dekker, a popular poet himself and so an interested party, positively suggested in a poem to King James I that some 'Adamantine Act' be made against these illiterate trespassers.[2] Amidst material of so many different kinds it is not easy to plot out a clear path or to hold to a single theme. Part of my purpose is to indicate the way in which these poems, singly or in groups, illuminate the events and policies of the time and sometimes influence them. I hope also, though necessarily in a more fragmentary and tentative way,

6

to say something of the development and characteristics of this kind of verse.

Satire has always been regarded with respect by critics and literary historians, and ballads have long been the object of antiquarian study; but I do not think that all politically inspired poetry has been treated before, as a whole, over this period, or that the more robust forms of political verse have been deliberately contrasted with and considered alongside the courtly verse of the time. In such wide pastures I shall certainly, now and then, miss my way, but I hope that this exploration may make up in incidental entertainment for what it lacks in direction, and will show that this country, lying admittedly only in the foothills of Parnassus, has an interest and value of its own. If I do no more in the following reflections, I may at least suggest some possible ideas and questions for future explorers to investigate.

In March 1603 Queen Elizabeth I died and it has become something of a platitude to say that the reign of King James was a sad falling off from that of his great predecessor, a time of disillusion and doubt, of increasing corruption and jockeying for place at Court, of unworthy financial shifts. But in the last years of Elizabeth the discontents of King James's reign in Court, country and Parliament were already present. Thus, the satires of John Donne

were not published until the reign of Charles I, and
described the problems and types of that later epoch
so well as to be wrily quoted by Wentworth and
others whose business lay with the Court, but they
had in fact been written before Queen Elizabeth
died. The courtier, so clearly drawn by Donne,
frequented the ante-rooms of Whitehall, Hampton
Court and Greenwich any time in the half century
from the 1590's to the early 1640's. The inefficiency
and intrigues of such men hastened the breakdown
of the monarchy. Donne thus describes a typical
place-hunting courtier:

> He knowes who loves; whom; and who by poyson
> Hasts to an Offices reversion;
> He knowes who' hath sold his land, and now doth beg
> A license, old iron, bootes, shooes, and egge-
> shels to transport; Shortly boyes shall not play
> At span-counter, or blow-point, but they pay
> Toll to some Courtier;...
> He names a price for every office paid;
> He saith, our warres thrive ill, because delai'd;
> That offices are entail'd, and that there are
> Perpetuities of them, lasting as farre
> As the last day; And that great officers
> Doe with the Pirates share, and Dunkirkers....[3]

Already in Queen Elizabeth's time monopolies
granted to courtiers were a major grievance, while
the sale and resale of the reversion of court offices
was cankering the central administration. Already
the financial practices which undermined the Stuart
throne honeycombed the Court like worm in the

wood. Only the most facile optimist hoped for radical changes in the new reign, but it is customary to expect improvement from alteration, and in fact the advent of the young king in place of the old queen was greeted with much more enthusiasm than is traditionally supposed. Queen Elizabeth's subjects sincerely mourned their glorious and remarkable sovereign, but her last years had been clouded with discontent, and much was hoped of her successor.

Thomas Dekker, essentially a popular poet, reflected a mood which was general:

> Blest God, when we for fear scarce looked to have seen Peace's moonshine
> Thou sends't from the North, past all our hopes, King James his glorious sunshine.

His sheaf of prose and verse on the year 1603, *The Wonderful Year*, is full of such things. On the coming of the king from Scotland he wrote:

> Silver Crowds
> Of blisful Angels and tryed Martyrs tread
> On the Star-seeling over *England*'s head:
> Now heaven broke into wonder, and brought forth
> Our *omne bonum* from the holesome North,
> (Our fruitfull Sovereigne) Iamus, at whose dread name
> Rebellion swounded, and (ere since) became
> Groveling and nerve-lesse, wanting bloud to nourish;
> For Ruin gnawes her selfe when kingdomes flourish.

There were certain solid causes for rejoicing. In the uncertain state of Europe it was as well to have

9

an assured succession, a lack which had constantly and rightly troubled the Parliaments of the childless Elizabeth. 'Our fruitful sovereign James', the father of two sons and a daughter, made the succession secure for the first time in the memory of most Englishmen. The union of the Crowns of England and Scotland was naturally expected to put an end, not only to troubles on the Border but to the potential danger which Scotland represented in English foreign policy. Dekker, in the same poem, is not altogether happy in the culinary pun which he applies to the king:

> Most blissfull Monarch of all earthen powers,
> Serv'd with a messe of kingdomes....[4]

The suggestion of the king devouring his kingdoms is, all things considered, not fortunate. More elegant, and more frequent in the complimentary verses of the time, is the marriage simile, expressed most happily by Ben Jonson:

> When was there contract better driven by *Fate*?
> And celebrated with more truth of state?
> The world the temple was, the priest a King,
> The spoused paire two realmes, the sea the ring.[5]

Samuel Daniel, in an immensely long poem of welcome to King James, thus hails the union:

> Shake hands with Union, O thou mighty State,
> Now thou art all *Great-Britaine* and no more,
> No Scot, no English now, nor no debate:
> No borders but the Ocean and the Shore:

No wall of *Adrian* serves to separate
Our mutuall love, nor our obedience,
Being subjects all to one Imperial Prince.

What heretofore could never yet be wrought
By all the swords of pow'r, by bloud, by fire,
By ruine and destruction; here is brought
To passe with peace, with love, with joy, desire:
Our former blessed union hath begot
A greater union that is more intire,
And makes us more our selves, sets us at one
With Nature that ordain'd us to be one.[6]

The wedding simile, extended, appears again, this time from a Scottish poet, Sir William Alexander:

And though our Nations, long I must confesse,
Did roughly woo before that they could wed;
That but endeers the Union we possesse,
When *Neptune* both confines within one bed:
All ancient injuries this doth redresse,
And buries that which many a battell bred;
  Brave discords reconcil'd (if wrath expire)
  Do breed the greatest love, and most intire....[7]

Sir William Alexander, later Earl of Stirling, was one of a group of Scots poets, which included Sir Robert Aytoun and Alexander Craig, who willingly lent their talents to the support of the king's ideal of a complete fusion of the two nations. The king would have liked to displace the terms England and Scotland—as suggested in Daniel's poem—for those of North and South Britain, the component parts of the joined nation of Great Britain. There was vague talk of elevating York into the new capital, but the

whole scheme foundered on the total unwillingness
of the English Commons to agree to an amalgamation of Parliaments.

There remained, none the less, this group of
Scottish writers who called themselves the Scoto-
Britanes and set the fashion—followed by all their
educated compatriots for the next century and
bitterly deplored since—for abandoning the already
highly developed qualities of their northern tongue
and writing in southern English.

One of them, Alexander Craig, is almost alarm-
ingly frank in an address to the king on his reasons
for coming to England to seek favour at Court:

> My rusticke Muse whenas each one cry'd out,
> Could not be heard from so remote a place....
> Wee come from farthest *Scotish* coastes to thee,
> Some portion of thy royall feast to finde:
> It restes in thee to welcome us therefore,
> And make me rich, that I may beg no more.[8]

The king's generous attempts to make his Scottish
followers rich were not popular in England and
sometimes reacted badly on their own country. Sir
William Alexander was rewarded with a patent for
making copper coins for Scotland, an enterprise
which caused a minor currency crisis so that he
came to be called in certain anonymous Scottish
pasquils 'Alexander the coppersmith'. The obvious
allusion to St Paul's second epistle to Timothy
would not be missed by anyone.

Enthusiasm for the union of the crowns faded very quickly in Scotland among all except those who had followed the Court. The king, who had promised to come back once in every three years, stayed away for fourteen years, causing some economic loss and far greater offence to his Scottish subjects, and laying up troubles of which his son was to feel the full weight. Alexander Craig, who had saluted the king with so much enthusiasm on his accession to the English Crown, had changed his note by the time the king came back to Scotland in 1617. The arguments with which he urged James not to leave Scotland a second time were as simple as they were sincere:

> Stay then (dread liege) O stay with us a while
> With pleasing sports the posting tyme begyle:
> Thy fynest Hawks and fleitest Hounds shall find
> Of fowls and beasts a pray of everie kynd....
> Throgh forests, Parks and fields hunt stag and Haire
> It helps the health to have the native air....
> Live *Nestors* dayes King James but live among us
> By blood and birth thou do'st alone belong us,
> Stay then at home, to *Thames* make no returne,
> Sleip with thy fathers in thy father's urn.[9]

The plea was disregarded; James never came back to Scotland, and it was sixteen more years before Scotland again saw her king. In the circumstances the welcome addressed to King Charles on his visit in 1633 by the plebeian poet William Lithgow is on the whole remarkable for its restraint. But he puts some significant lines into the mouth of Scotland:

> True, and most true it is, the Proverb proves,
> That age is still injur'd by younger loves:
> And so am I, thine eldest *Region* made,
> A prey to dark oblivion's winter-shade.

The neglected and forgotten Scotland goes on to deplore the magnetism that the English Court now exercises over her great men:

> My *Lords* they post up dayly to thy *Court*
> And ly there Months and Yeares; and doe resort
> To *London*, as their Livings lay and Land,
> In midst of *Cheapsyde*, *King Streete*, or the *Strand*....
> Still up and downe they make a play of Posting,
> And laugh at lavish expence; fall a boasting
> Who oftest courts thy *Court*, whilst here at home
> Their *Wives* and *Children* cry, When will they come?
> Yea, yea, they come, but with an empty hand,
> And to turne back, morgadging heere more land:
> Wherein I vow, that *England* turnes a curse
> To mee, and my spent *Gentry*, and their Purse.[10]

Such, in the estimation of the Scots, was the fate of their country. Meanwhile their truant king was trying experiments in England. King James, when he first came south, had set himself an ideal of government which was in many ways admirable: an ideal of order at home and peace abroad, from which, presently, all other good things would flow. He never fully grasped that he had neither the statesmanship nor the resources to achieve his goal: but that is too complex a problem to discuss here.

In one of the earliest masques to be presented at his Court in England, Samuel Daniel very prettily celebrated the royal ideal of government. Iris the messenger of the Gods appeared to tell the audience that the isles of Greece were now 'nests of barbarism and spoil' and that the Gods had, therefore, decided to 'recreate themselves upon the western mount of mighty Brittane, the land of civil musick and of rest'. At this sign twelve goddesses descended one by one, and uttered in turn sage quatrains about peace, concord, unity, prosperity and sea-power. In this lightly didactic masque, the queen, blonde empty-headed Anne of Denmark, elected to present Pallas Athene, a choice of part which would have made her husband smile if he had been listening. But King James was frankly indifferent to this kind of entertainment, inclined to fall asleep at masques, and sometimes later in life to lose patience and stop the entertainment in the middle. This may be the reason that all trace of political significance vanishes from later masques. The famous combined works of Ben Jonson and Inigo Jones were spectacles with no didactic content, well suited to the rather pompous frivolity of the queen and her ladies.

Daniel's *Twelve Goddesses* had, none the less, pointed the way to a propagandist use of the masque which was to return as the king's younger son, Charles, grew up, and which was to be the accepted mode when he became king. Charles inherited his mother's passion for masquing and something of her taste for presenting parts for which he was not altogether suited; in his reign he used the masque with almost tiresome reiteration to underline and point out the beauties of his policy.

King James's conception of policy was impressive on paper. This was especially true of his foreign policy, for he saw himself as the God-directed peace-maker of Europe. At the time of his accession to the English throne, the wars engendered by the Reformation had been violently renewed. The crusading influence of Jesuits and Capucins dominated many Catholic European princes, and a generation of religious statesmen had grown up ready to pursue and carry to a final outcome the work of the Counter-Reformation.

The united kingdom of Great Britain, lying on the perimeter of Europe, was of considerable strategic importance as an ally either for the Roman Catholic or the Protestant powers. Rightly or wrongly, the majority of the king's articulate subjects believed their country's place in the European struggle to be with the Protestant powers. But King James made peace with Spain and committed his people to neutrality. The obvious advantages of this period of tranquillity were not at all so obvious to a people who, quite apart from a sincere desire to assist their Protestant co-religionists in the struggle with the Whore of Babylon, were concerned to break down Spanish sea-power, still dominant in the West Indies and threatening in the English Channel, and to make way for their own expansion.

This popular English view was very crude, but it was widespread; it was a cardinal weakness of the Stuart kings, throughout the century, that they never made allowance for the vehemence of their people's prejudices and the force of their political ideas. Time and time again these prejudices and passions spill over into popular doggerel and ballad verse. They were expressed too in the works of more ambitious poets and more educated men. Such was the intensity and persistence of anti-Spanish feeling that Richard Crashaw, whose friends were after all men of education and of Roman Catholic sympathies, thought it necessary to excuse his devotion to Saint Teresa, and almost to excuse Saint Teresa herself, because of the unfortunate and inescapable fact that she was a Spaniard:

> Let no fond hate
> Of names and words so farre prejudicate;
> Soules are not Spaniards too, one frendly flood
> Of Baptisme, blends them all into a blood.
> Christs Faith makes but one body of all soules,
> And loves that bodyies soul; no Law controules
> Our free trafick for heaven, we may maintaine,
> Peace sure with piety, though it dwell in *Spaine*.
> What soul soever in any Language can
> Speake heaven like hers, is my soules countryman.[11]

Early in King James's reign the Gunpowder Plot gave enormous encouragement to the popular belief in the machinations of the Jesuits. They were believed to lurk in every European community secretly or openly hammering out their wicked designs, 'for Rome's use on Spanish anvil' as Phineas Fletcher categorically states in a poem directed against them and called *The Apollyonists*. The Gunpowder Plot was thought to be all their work, part of a deep-laid design to gain possession of 'this little isle', this blessed plot of ground hitherto free from Spain and popery. Time and again England had been saved, as it seemed by Providence, from the engulfing maw of popish Spain—once when at the time of her Spanish marriage Mary Tudor proved blessedly barren; and again even more dramatically, in her sister Elizabeth's reign, when the Armada was defeated. The Gunpowder Plot was hailed as another providential deliverance. The intensity of this widespread fear comes out in several poems on the Plot, some by intelligent and distinguished writers. Crashaw incidentally made no less than three attempts at a Gunpowder Plot poem.

Of particular interest is the long passage devoted to the Plot in Phineas Fletcher's *Apollyonists*. Fletcher had rather simple political views, but it is worth emphasising that he was neither stupid nor uneducated. A scholar of Eton and a Fellow of King's, he was also the son of an experienced diplomat. His poem, however ingenuously it reflects on policy, is well informed on facts. Several verses are devoted to events in Russia (where his father had been the English envoy); he described the recent Polish–Russian war and the adventures of that strange pretender the pseudo-Demetrius. But when he came to the Gunpowder Plot, Fletcher wrote with a simplicity worthy of a medieval mystery play. The scene is Hell and a council of fiends is in session, among them the Spirit of Ignatius Loyola, who speaks:

> That blessed Isle, so often curst in vaine,
> Triumphing in our losse and idle spight,
> Of force shall shortly stoop to Rome and Spayne:
> I'le take a way ne're knowne to man or spright.
> To kill a King is stale, and I disdaine:
> That fits a Secular, not a Jesuite.
> Kings, Nobles, Clergy, Commons high and low,
> The Flowre of England in one houre I'le mow,
> And 'head all th' Isle in one unseen, unfenced blow.

He then describes the

> Cellars large, and caverns vaulted deep
> With bending arches borne, and columnes strong

which support the Parliament house, and how he will slyly creep in there

> And when with numbers just the house gins swell,
> And every state hath fill'd his station,
> When now the King mounted on lofty sell,
> With honyed speech and comb'd oration
> Charms every eare, midst of that sugred spell
> I'le teare the walls, blow up the nation,

> Bullet to Heaven the stones with thunders loud,
> Equall to th' earth the courts, and turrets proud,
> And fire the shaking towne, and quench't with
>   royall blood.[12]

If intelligent men could feel as Fletcher did about Spain, Jesuits and the Pope, it was not surprising that the popular hopes which the king had inspired at his first coming dwindled when he initiated a policy of friendship towards Spain. The disappointed shifted their attention to the heir apparent, Prince Henry, whose principal charm in the eyes of the public was his warlike temperament. When he jousted at Court on Twelfth Night 1610, Ben Jonson, in verses written for the occasion, compared him to Richard Cœur de Lion, Edward I and Henry V. Sir William Alexander called him a new Black Prince:

> Thou, like that gallant Thunder-bolt of warre,
> Third *Edwards* sonne, who was so much renown'd,
> Shalt shine in valour as the morning starre,
> And plenish with thy praise the peopled round;
> But like to his, let nought thy fortune marre,
> Who, in his Fathers time, did dye uncrown'd....[13]

The comparison was all too just. Prince Henry died in November 1612, at the age of eighteen, or, as the same poet laboriously put it, 'when the spheres and muses joined did serve to count his years'.

The prince's death was greeted with deep and genuine lamentation. Elegies and epitaphs were written by Jonson, Donne, Chapman, Drummond,

Herbert of Cherbury, Campion, Heywood, Sylvester and many lesser men. But all that truly could be said was summed up in four lines of an epitaph doubtfully attributed to Ben Jonson:

> Within this marble casket lies,
> A matchlesse jewell of rich prize,
> Whom Nature in the worlds disdaine,
> But shewd, and then put up againe.[14]

The prince had died before anything except vague and general hopes could be expressed about him. But such political comment or prophecy as there is in the elegies for him is all of one kind. He was chiefly regretted because, unlike his father, he was warlike. Drummond of Hawthornden went as far as to regret that, since the prince had to die, he did not die, like the Connétable de Bourbon, in the very act of conquering Rome. The Eternal City would thus have become the scene of his triumph and his tomb[15]—an ambition as unrealistic as it appears to us unseemly.

Tears were rapidly dried between Prince Henry's death in the autumn of 1612 and the marriage of his sister, Princess Elizabeth, to the Elector Palatine of the Rhine on St Valentine's Day 1613, for which Donne wrote an enchanting Epithalamium. The popular enthusiasm for a royal wedding was powerfully strengthened by the belief that this marriage to a Protestant prince betokened a change of policy. It did not in fact mean anything of the kind. It was only a part of the king's strangely unrealistic scheme for establishing himself as the arbiter of Europe by marrying his daughter to a leading Protestant prince and—in due course—his son to a Spanish princess.

In 1618 the uneasy truce which had prevailed in Europe during the second decade of the century was brought to an end by the revolt of the Protestants of Bohemia who offered the Crown to James's son-in-law Frederick. Frederick was, through his mother, the grandson of William the Silent, the liberator of the Netherlands. The enemies of the Habsburg dynasty hoped that history would repeat itself and the revolt of Bohemia prove as threatening to their power in Central Europe as the revolt of the Netherlands had been to them in northern Europe fifty years earlier. This parallel between Frederick, the Protestant king of Bohemia, and William the Silent did much to heighten the hopes of zealous Protestants.

With the Bohemian revolt began the last phase of the religious wars which had troubled Europe since the Reformation, wars in which a majority of King James's subjects were anxious that their country should take arms, partly out of rivalry with Spain but mostly from a genuine and justified fear of a Catholic reconquest of northern Europe.

We are to-day rather too insular in our attitude to the seventeenth century, concentrating on the interesting domestic developments of our country at this period—on the struggle for power between the Crown and the gentry, and especially on its legal, constitutional, economic and social aspects. It is an understandable failing, since the conflict was to be in its ultimate outcome for the English-speaking world far more important than anything that happened in the coeval German Thirty Years War. But to our ancestors, events in Europe were believed, not without cause, to affect the fate of England closely, and the struggle of their Protestant co-religionists on the continent was watched with profound and justified anxiety. The king's unwillingness or inability to intervene effectively on the Protestant side did irreparable damage to the prestige and popularity of the Crown. His son-in-law, Frederick, suffered a lamentable overthrow in Bohemia, and by the end of 1620 not only Bohemia but most of south Germany was controlled by Austrian and Bavarian armies while Protestants were everywhere in flight. Spanish troops had occupied the Rhineland and the Dutch were girding themselves for a war to the death to preserve their gravely threatened independence.

The agitations, anxieties and hopes of the English during these months were reflected in the current publications of popular writers. Thomas Dekker came out with *Dekker his Dreame*, an apocalyptic vision of the end of the world, that faithfully summed up contemporary feelings. The German princes, divided in religion, quarrelling and fickle, allowed the flood of Spanish–Austrian Catholic forces to sweep over their land, while the Protestant powers, uncertain and divided by political-theological quarrels, seemed unable to stand against them:

> The Sacred Empire did it Selfe o'rewhelme;
> State on state trampled; realm did beat down realme:
> Religion (all this while) a Garment wore,
> Stayn'd like a Painter's Apron, and turn'd Whore
> To severall Countries, till from deepe Abysme
> Up her Two Bastards came (Error and Schisme),
> She in That motley Cloake, with her Two Twinnes,
> Travell'd from land to land, sowing Ranck Sinnes,
> Which choak'd the Good Corne, and from them did rise
> Opinions, factions, black leav'd Heresies;
> Pride, Superstition, Rancour, Hate, Disdaine,
> So that (me thought) on earth no good did Reigne....[16]

But King James held obstinately to the belief that the European situation would yield to diplomacy and that he could ultimately mediate a peace by marrying his son to the Infanta of Spain. That misguided policy culminated in the visit of Prince Charles and the Duke of Buckingham to Spain to fetch home the bride. But the prince and the duke returned without the Infanta, convinced of the duplicity of the Spanish government and openly determined to break off the alliance. This revolution of affairs was hailed with enthusiasm by the London populace and made even the Duke of Buckingham briefly into a hero.

The Court masque, prepared for the following Christmas by Ben Jonson, was the first for many years to have any political content. It was called *Neptune's Triumph for Albion's Return*, and Prince Charles was to figure in the character of Albion. The text opens with a dialogue in which the author is attacked for having waited so long to utter his welcome to the Prince: Charles had reached England in October and it is now Twelfth Night. The poet answers that he did not wish his more elegant lines to compete with 'th'abortive and extemporal din of balladry' which had greeted the prince's home-coming; he had preferred to delay until 'every song-ster had sung out his fit'. The theme of the masque—which is pointed by an anti-masque of sailors crying 'Hey for our young Master!'—is the joy of Neptune at the return of the young prince who will hence-forth see to it that Britain rules the waves. The emphasis on sea-power was exactly in tune with the views of Prince Charles himself at this time and of Buckingham; it was also the popular view. It ran counter to the old king's wishes. If he could no longer hope for peace, he still hoped for a contained land war which would put him to no more cost than that of sending a small expeditionary force to the Rhineland. But the old king was saved from any embarrassment the masque might have caused him because it was not, in the end, presented. A quarrel about precedence arose between the Spanish and

French ambassadors which made it necessary to curtail the festivities altogether and call it off. It is reasonable to suspect that the Spanish ambassador worked up this argument over protocol because he, even less than the king, relished a masque glorifying English sea-power.

The doomed and useless negotiations for the Spanish marriage dragged slowly to an inglorious end while Martin Parker, London's most popular ballad-monger, came out with a consoling doggerel to assure King James's subjects that their sovereign's heart was in the right place:

> The Pope he excludeth,
> Though oft he intrudeth:
> Yet like zealous *Iudeth*,
> his head he will crop:
> Like good *Hezekias*,
> And fervent *Josias*,
> He serves the *Messias*,
> and hateth the Pope.[17]

While this kind of ditty was sung in the streets, the Spanish ambassador protested against a theatrical performance in August of the same year. This was Middleton's *Game at Chess* in which the Anglo-Spanish negotiations were presented under the transparent disguise of a *Game at Chess* which concluded with the triumph of the White Knight (Prince Charles) and the White Duke (Buckingham) over the Black King, Queen, Knight and Bishop and any number of pawns. This rather laboured piece played to full houses for over a week (a long run for those days) with takings of as much as a hundred pounds a night before the infuriated ambassador at length got the King's Council to intervene. The author vanished temporarily from London and the rest of the company humbled themselves before the Council table and took off the offending play.

The play is not a very exact account of the facts, but it contains passages which very clearly reflect the popular view of contemporary politics. The Jesuits are throughout the villains, the moving spirits of Black, or Spanish, policy. At one point the White Knight and Duke, Charles and Buckingham, enter the house of the Black King (Philip IV) in pretended friendship in order to ambush and entrap him. While there, they are entertained at a banquet at which the Black Knight (who stands for Olivarez, the King of Spain's *privado* and chief minister), describes in succulent terms how his master has devoured the world:

And in the large feast of our vast ambition
We count but the White Kingdom, whence you come from,
The garden for our cook to pick his salads;
The food's lean France, larded with Germany;
Before which comes the grave, chaste signiory
Of Venice, serv'd in, capon-like, in white broth;
From our chief oven, Italy, the bake-meats;
Savoy the salt, Geneva the chipt manchet;
Below the salt the Netherlands are placed,
A common dish at lower end o' the table

> For meaner pride to fall to; for our second course,
> A spit of Portugals serv'd in for plovers;
> Indians and Moors for blackbirds; all this while
> Holland stands ready melted to make sauce
> On all occasions.

The White Knight, Prince Charles, here breaks in:

> Here's meat enough, in conscience, for ambition!

Olivarez continues:

> If there be any want, there's Switzerland,
> Polonia, and such pickled things will serve
> To furnish our table.[18]

The joke was grim enough because, whatever else in the play was groundless, this list of places under the domination of Spain or her Austrian allies was by no means exaggerated; indeed more could have been added: Middleton puts in Poland as the pickles and Holland as the sauce (it is interesting to find this early reference to sauce Hollandaise) but why does he omit Bohemia? I can only suppose that he left it out because the defeat of the Winter-King, Frederick, and his wife, the princess of England, made it too painful a subject for his audience.

Jonson's ill-fated masque, this play of Middleton's and the ephemeral ballads which greeted the prince's return, show that popular writers, ballad-mongers and Court poets were all united against the king's policy, and had all become vocal under the sheltering protection of the heir apparent and the Duke of Buckingham. But whatever his failure in foreign policy, the old king's last sickness was commemorated by at least one Court poet, Thomas Carew, in a manner which showed that James's frequent lectures to his ministers and his courtiers on the meaning of sovereignty had not gone unheeded. In *The True Law of Free Monarchies* the king had written:

The King towards his people is rightly compared to a father of children and to a head of a body composed of divers members...and as there is ever hope of curing any diseased member by the direction of the head, as long as it is whole; but by the contrary, if it be troubled, all the members are partakers of that pain, so is it betwixt the prince and his people.[19]

Carew takes this up in a poem which most strangely describes the effect of the king's last illness on the Court:

> Entring his royal limbs that is our head,
> Through us his mystique limbs the paine is spread,
> That man that doth not feele his part, hath none
> In any part of his dominion;
> If he hold land, that earth is forfeited,
> And he unfit on any ground to tread.
> This griefe is felt at Court, where it doth move
> Through every joynt, like the true soule of love.
> All those faire starres that doe attend on Him,
> Whence they deriv'd their light, wax pale and dim.
> That ruddie morning beame of Majestie,
> Which should the Suns eclipsed light supply,

Is overcast with mists, and in the liew
Of cheerfull rayes sends us downe drops of dew:
That curious forme made of an earth refin'd,
At whose blest birth, the gentle Planets shin'd
With faire aspects, and sent a glorious flame
To animate so beautifull a frame;
That Darling of the Gods and men, doth weare
A cloude on's brow, and in his eye a teare:
And all the rest, (save when his dread command
Doth bid them move,) like livelesse statues stand;
So full a griefe, so generally worne
Shewes a good King is sick and good men mourne.[20]

These laboured lines illustrate a tendency which was to be powerfully exaggerated in the ensuing reign, the reign of that prince 'made of an earth refin'd at whose blest birth the gentle planets shined'. Carew has in this poem very elaborately developed an idea which was an important part of the king's own conception of his office and handed it back to him ingeniously versified. This habit of the Court poets, and later also of the university wits if they happened to be of the king's way of thinking, was to be typical of the next reign. Frequent poetic exercises in this vein undoubtedly had the effect of inducing a self-complacent and self-congratulatory attitude in the king and in some of his closest friends. Trivial in themselves, the compliments of the Court poets were not in the end to be quite so trivial in their results: they stimulated, both in those who wrote and in those who received them, an attitude of mind which weakened the judgment and made king and courtiers alike unable to read the harsher signs of the times. It is wiser for a ruler to listen to the vulgar exaggerations of popular ballad politics than to attend only to graceful compliments.

King James died of the sickness which inspired Thomas Carew's lines, and in March 1625 his son ascended the throne, amid a general belief that he would embark on that war for the expansion of British sea-power and the Protestant cause in Europe for which so many of his subjects hoped. Phineas Fletcher, voicing the typical patriotic Protestant outlook, apostrophised him thus:

> But thou, Greate Prince, in whose successefull raigne,
> Thy Britanes 'gin renue their Martiall fame,
> Our Soveraigne Lord, our joy more Soveraigne,
> Our onely Charles, under whose ominous name
> Rome wounded first, still pines in ling'ring paine;
> Thou who hast seen, and loath'd Romes whorish shame,
>   Rouse those brave Sparkes, which in thy bosome swell,
>   Cast downe this second Lucifer to hell:
> So shalt thou all thy Sires, so shalt thy selfe excell.
>
> 'Tis not in vaine, that Christ hath girt thy head
> With three fayre peacefull Crownes; 'tis not in vaine,
> That in thy Realmes such spirits are dayly bred,
> Which thirst, and long to tug with Rome, and Spayne...
>   Here, noble Charles, enter thy chevalrie;
>   The Eagle scornes at lesser game to flie;
> Onely this warres a match worthy thy Realmes, and Thee.
>
> Ah happy man, that lives to see that day!
> Ah happy man, who in that warre shall bleed!
> Happy who beares the standard in that fray!
> Happy who quells the rising Babel seed!

Thrice happy who that whore shall doubly pay!
This (royall Charles) this be thy happy meed.
Mayst thou that triple diademe trample downe,
This shall thy name in earth, and Heaven renowne,
And adde to these three here, there a thrice triple crowne.[21]

The emphasis on the triple crown of England, Scotland and Ireland, against the Pope's triple crown, is an interesting and typical piece of seventeenth-century symbolism. The contrast is not merely a rhetorical device; such ideas had meanings to our forefathers which have been lost to us. Many of the king's subjects probably did feel that there was some special force, or at least some portent, in the three-in-one character which, since 1603, had been assumed by their sovereign, a character which reflected the religious conception of the Trinity.

Phineas Fletcher must have written these lines shortly after the new king's accession, when aggressive and blood-thirsty hopes were being widely canvassed. They were published in 1627, just after the disastrous naval expedition to Cadiz, just before the equally disastrous attempt by Buckingham to relieve the French Protestants besieged at La Rochelle. Very soon it would be apparent that the popular hopes which sprang up at King Charles's accession were to be disappointed, as the hopes aroused by King James in 1603 had also been disappointed. But in the reign of King James the Court poets at least had always found some figure near the king to whom they could attach their conventional, though not necessarily insincere, views of their country's power and glory. Prince Henry and later Prince Charles had been the rising stars on whom Court poets as well as popular ballad-mongers could fix their attention.

In King James's reign, therefore, there was no serious divergence in matter, but only in manner, between popular ballads on political or royal themes, and the more sophisticated Court productions. Thomas Carew's poem on the king's sickness (not published until some years later) is the first clear indication of something different. The lines would be incomprehensible to the vulgar and the theme is remote from ordinary day to day political speculation. It foreshadows a division between the Court attitude and the popular attitude which was rapidly to widen in the next fifteen years. In the reign of Charles I, the political divisions of the nation assumed menacing shape, and were echoed alike by the poets of the Court, the universities, and the London streets. The conflict would broaden the range and increase the striking power of English political verse.

II

THE HALCYON DAYS

Few epochs in our history have been saluted by contemporary poets with so much courtly gaiety, or mourned with so much lyrical tenderness, as the decade which preceded the Civil War. The 1630's, that blessed time of peace, seen through the smoke and smother of the ensuing years of Civil War, acquired a magical beauty even for those who had not at the time been in close sympathy with the royal government. Andrew Marvell was twenty when the Civil War broke out; he can have known little about the personal rule of King Charles and his sympathies were not with the Cavaliers. None the less he subscribed to the idealised view of the 1630's, and in his lovely poem on the house and garden of Fairfax, the Parliamentarian general, sincerely lamented their passing:

> Oh Thou, that dear and happy Isle
> The Garden of the World ere while,
> Thou *Paradise* of four Seas,
> Which *Heaven* planted us to please,
> But, to exclude the World, did guard
> With watry if not flaming Sword;
> What luckless Apple did we tast,
> To make us Mortal, and Thee Wast?[22]

34

Abraham Cowley, who had been just old enough
to enjoy the last palmy days of peace and who supported King Charles with devotion, did not achieve
so perfect a simplification of the picture. In his
anxiety to supply concrete examples of the benefits of
the royal rule he congested his lines with economic
and social facts; or if not facts, then at least opinions,
since it was (and is) more generally held that the
epoch he depicts as prosperous was a time of
economic depression. Inaccurate he may be, but he
is sincere in his yearning regret for the blessed days
of King Charles. What, he asked, had made England
fall into Civil War and turn her back on a time

> When all the riches of the Globe beside
> Flow'd into Thee with every Tide;
> When all that Nature did thy Soil deny,
> The Growth was of thy fruitfull Industry,
> When all the proud and dreadfull Sea,
> And all his Tributary-streams,
> A constant Tribute paid to Thee.
> When all the liquid World was one extended Thames....
>
> When Men to Men respect and friendship bore,
> And God with Reverence did adore;
> When upon Earth no Kingdom could have shown
> A happier Monarch to us than our own....[23]

Statements made, not in retrospect but by contemporary poets attached to the Court, were much
like these later idealisations. The courtiers frequently
congratulated the king and themselves on the era
of peace and plenty that he had inaugurated, and

compared the tranquillity of England in the midst of European wars to the peace which the halcyon bird is supposed to create amid the raging of the sea.

Peace and plenty were, strangely enough, not the popular ideal in politics at this epoch, nor in the opening years of King Charles's reign were they the objects of his policy. In 1625 when he came to the throne, he and the all-powerful Buckingham were still both in agreement with the people in wanting war with Spain and planning the resurgence of English sea-power. Martin Parker's popular ballad of about 1625 with its refrain 'Come let us to the warres againe' was much more to the taste not only of the London populace but also of the young king. Conquest and expansion are the openly admitted motives for fighting; religion is added as an after-thought:

> *France* and *Flanders* makes no mone,
> they get riches, we get none,
> Flemish Captaines sayle about,
> unknowne Islands to find out:...
> The true Religion to maintaine,
> Come let us to the warres againe.

> The *Germane* States, and Netherlands,
> have mustred up their martiall bands:
> The *Denmarke* King doth close combine,
> his forces to the *Palatine*:
> With three hundred princes more,
> 'side Dukes, Earles and Barons store:
> Then how can we at home remaine,
> But bravely to those warres againe.[24]

This was very far from the tone of the tranquil 1630's. Between the king's accession in 1625 and his decision to rule without further reference to Parliament in 1629, the Court circle lost all taste for war because of the failure of the naval expeditions to Cadiz and La Rochelle. The king and Court blamed the failure on the unwillingness of Parliament to grant adequate supplies; but majority opinion in the country, both educated and popular, rightly or wrongly blamed it on mismanagement at the top, and on the ineptitude above all of Buckingham. Even men otherwise devotedly loyal to the king shared the dislike and contempt for the favourite. Thus so faithful a Royalist as Drummond in one of those privately circulated epigrams which, with other lampoons on the duke, were very common at the time, commented on the first unsuccessful expedition to La Rochelle:

> Charles, would yee quaile your foes, have better lucke;
> Send forth some Drakes, and keep at home the Ducke.[25]

The murder of the duke followed shortly afterwards, in August 1628. The general feeling of relief could not, for evident reasons, be freely expressed, although, only a few weeks before Buckingham's death, Martin Parker had celebrated with callous enthusiasm the brutal killing of one of his henchmen, Dr Lamb, by a gang of sailors:

> The fourteenth day of June
> Which was upon a Friday,

> In the afternoone,
> We may count it a high-day,
> for what was done.... [26]

He and most of his readers thought it even more of a high day when the duke himself was the victim; but what could be freely written of the relatively insignificant Dr Lamb could not be openly said of the king's favourite and first minister. The published ballads on Buckingham are therefore conventional; they concentrate for the most part on the age-old theme of the uncertainty of life even for great men. Court comment was markedly different. Thomas Carew's poetic epitaph is typical:

> When in the brazen leaves of Fame,
> The life, the death, of *Buckingham*
> Shall be recorded, if Truth's hand
> Incize the story of our Land,
> Posteritie shall see a faire
> Structure, by the studious care
> Of two Kings rays'd, that did no lesse
> Their wisdome, than their Power expresse;
> By blinded zeale (whose doubtfull light
> Made murders scarlet robe seeme white,
> Whose vain-deluding phantosmes charm'd
> A clouded, sullen soule, and arm'd
> A desperate hand, thirstie of blood)
> Torne from the faire earth where it stood;
> So the majestique fabrique fell.
> His Actions let our Annals tell:
> Wee write no Chronicle; This Pile
> Weares onely sorrowes face and stile.... [27]

On the whole posterity has not fulfilled Carew's hope that the wisdom of King James and King

Charles would be highly praised for their patronage of Buckingham; but the 'clouded, sullen soul' is an apt description of John Felton his murderer. One other courtly epitaph is worth quoting, that composed by James Shirley, because it is of a type—a series of balanced statements in contradiction or complement to each other—which was to be developed by other writers and for different, more famous epitaphs.

> Here lies the best and worst of Fate,
> Two Kings' delight, the people's hate,
> The Courtiers's star, the Kingdom's eye,
> A man to draw an Angel by,
> Fear's despiser, *Villiers* glory,
> The Great mans volume, all time's story.[28]

Apart from the fourth line it does not ring very true; but the portraits of Buckingham, with his noble forehead, his splendid eyes, his mane of silky hair, do show him indeed to have been a man 'to draw an angel by'.

So far the public utterances on the duke's death, but in that underworld and undergrowth of literature, where lampoons were privately circulated in manuscript, harsh things were said of Buckingham. Several unsigned mock elegies and epitaphs have survived, which combine extravagant praise of the murderer with condemnation of the duke. In contrast to Shirley's reverent epitaph, this venomous one is also, like Shirley's, built on double and balanced statements. Buckingham is speaking in the grave:

> I that my countrey did betray,
> Undid that King that let mee sway
> His sceptre as I pleas'd; brought downe
> The glorie of the English crowne;
> The courtiers' bane, the countries hate,
> An agent for the Spanish state;
> The Romists' frend, the Gospells foe,
> The Church and kingdomes overthrowe;
> Heere a damnéd carcase dwell,
> 'Till my soul returne from hell.
> With Judas then I shall inherit,
> Such portion as all traytors meritt.
> If heaven admitt of treason, pride, and lust,
> Expect my spotted soule among the just.[29]

After Buckingham's death the king was out of love with his war policy. Eighteen months later he got rid of his third Parliament without coming to any agreement with it, reversed all his warlike designs, made peace with Spain and France and settled down to create within the British Isles what had always been his father's ideal—a peaceful, prosperous, well-ordered government at home and no complications abroad. His decision was beautifully celebrated in verse by Richard Fanshawe who contrasted the happy state of the British Isles in 1630 with the troubles which raged abroad:

> The great *Gustavus* in the west
> Plucks the Imperiall Eagle's wing,
> Than whom the earth did ne'er invest
> A fiercer King.

> Revenging lost *Bohemia*,
> And the proud wrongs which Tilly did
> And tempereth the German clay
>   With Spanish bloud.
>
> What should I tell of Polish Bands,
> And the blouds boyling in the North?
> Gainst whom the furied Russians
>   Their Troops bring forth.

In contrast to all this in England—

> White Peace (the beautiful'st of things)
> Seems here her everlasting rest
> To fix, and spreads her downy wings
>   Over the nest.
>
> As when great *Jove* usurping Reigne
> From the plagu'd world did her exile,
> And ty'd her with a golden chaine
>   To one blest isle:
>
> Which in a sea of plenty swamme
> And Turtles sang on ev'ry bowgh,
> A safe retreat to all that came
>   As ours is now....[30]

The poem is the counterpart in words of Rubens' picture 'The Blessings of Peace', that rich and sensuous allegory which he painted for the king, while he was in London as ambassador from the Spanish Netherlands, in the same year in which this poem was written.

Another element now made its appearance which was not without significance in the royal policy.

The queen (Henrietta Maria to us, but to her contemporaries always Queen Mary) had lived very
much in the shadows while Buckingham dominated
her husband; she became soon after the favourite's
death of equal importance with the king in moulding
the character of their elegant Court and in shaping
the policy of the Crown. In the same year, 1630, the
year in which Fanshawe wrote the poem I have just
quoted, the year in which peace was made abroad,
she gave birth to her first living child. One little
known poet, angling rather openly for Court favour,
hailed this son of a British king and a French
princess as an emblem of peace between the kings
of Great Britain and France, who were after all
brothers-in-law, and of King Charles's return to the
conciliatory policy of the late King James:

> The Gods dear Issue, our greate Jove's increase;
> An Infant Embleme of his Grandsires peace;
> A Prince, th' happy mothers pretty smiler;
> The fathers and the uncles reconciler....[31]

For the Christmas festivities of 1630–1, Aurelian
Townshend wrote the masque which the king and
his lords performed. It was called *Albion's Triumph*,
a name reminiscent of Ben Jonson's ill-fated masque
Neptune's Triumph in Albion's Return in which eight
years before, to please the then warlike Charles, he
had shown him as potential conqueror of the sea
and the hope and darling of the navy. Now, Charles's
naval projects were in abeyance for lack of money,

and *Albion's Triumph* (Neptune had dropped out of it) was of a different kind—

> 'Tis not the Laurel Tree that brings,
> Anointing Oyle for sacred Kings:
> Those Princes see the happiest Dayes,
> Whose Olive Branches stand for Bayes....

Such is the gentle theme of Townshend's masque, in which Inigo Jones arranged for Peace, suitably attired, to descend from the clouds, while the closing chorus saluted the happy king and queen as 'Hymen's twin the Mary-Charles'.[32]

Two months later on Shrove Tuesday the queen and her ladies presented another masque, also written by Townshend, and called *Tempe Restored*. In this the deceiving enchantments of Circe are broken by the joint power of Heroic Virtue (meaning the king) and Divine Beauty personated, of course, by the queen's majesty.[33] The Court was gradually shutting itself up in a world of delighted self-congratulation into which the noisy politics of Europe were permitted to penetrate only in polite disguise.

When the king made peace with Spain, his subjects at first acquiesced in his defection from the Protestant Cause in Europe. They were resigned to a somewhat inglorious peace partly because they did not relish a war which had proved neither glorious nor profitable, and partly because the Protestant cause had, in 1630, a sufficient champion in the

King of Sweden, Gustavus Adolphus. But in
November 1632 Gustavus Adolphus was killed at
the battle of Lützen, an event which profoundly
perturbed all those who were concerned lest the
Spanish–Austrian power should again dominate
Europe, and penetrated even the enclosed peace of
the English Court. Townshend appealed to Thomas
Carew, who had recently distinguished himself with
an elegy on Dr Donne, to drop some more of his
ambrosial tears for the King of Sweden—

> So when the windes from every corner bring
> The too true nuse of the dead conquering King,
> Lett our land waters meeting by consent
> The showres descending from the Firmament,
> Make a new floode....[34]

Carew refused, and in his refusal summed up with
great felicity the mood of make-believe and play-
acting which was to be the undoing of King
Charles:

> But let us that in myrtle bowers sit
> Under secure shades, use the benefit
> Of peace and plenty, which the blessed hand
> Of our good King gives this obdurate Land,
> Let us of Revels sing, and let thy breath
> (Which filled Fames trumpet with *Gustavus* death,
> Blowing his name to heaven) gently inspire
> Thy past'rall pipe....
>
> Tourneyes, Masques, Theaters, better become
> Our *Halcyon* dayes; what though the German Drum
> Bellow for freedome and revenge, the noyse
> Concernes not us, nor should divert our joyes;

> Nor ought the thunder of their Carabins
> Drowne the sweet Ayres of our tun'd Violins;
> Beleeve me friend, if their prevailing powers
> Gaine them a calme securitie like ours,
> They'le hang their Armes up on the Olive bough,
> And dance, and revell then, as we doe now.[35]

The artificially induced legend of the calm and happy 1630's, the blissful days of King Charles's personal rule, is seen here fully and firmly established. But it was chiefly at Court that this vision of a peaceful land with, according to Fanshawe, turtles singing on every bough, was nourished and sustained. A faint note of doubt here and there suggests that even the most eloquent of the poetic propagandists for this idea were not always quite happy about it. Carew spoke of the blessed hand of our good king giving peace to 'this obdurate land'. Ben Jonson, who was far too perceptive a man not to know that popular feeling was rising against the king, had written in this vein:

> How happy were the subject, if he knew,
> Most pious King, but his own good in you....
> Indeed, when had Great Britain greater cause
> Than now to love the sovereign and the laws?

After enumerating the king's virtues rather conventionally he ended with a condemnation of the nation's ingratitude:

> How is she barren grown of love, or broke,
> That nothing can her gratitude provoke!

O times, o manners, surfeit bred of ease
The truly epidemical desease!
Tis not alone the merchant but the clown,
Is bankrupt turn'd; the cassock, cloak and gown
Are lost upon account; and none will know
How much to heaven for thee, great Charles, they owe.[36]

The king and queen, not unnaturally, preferred the work of poets who did not draw attention to the deplorable ingratitude of their subjects. Foremost among these was the dramatist and poet James Shirley, whose plays the king much admired. Early in 1634 Shirley wrote the most famous and the most expensive masque of the decade. It was put on, not by the king, but by the lawyers of the Inns of Court, and presented to the king and queen as a spectacular way of repudiating one of their number, the Puritan barrister William Prynne who in his famous attack on stage plays had, or was supposed to have, reflected on the queen's performance in Court masques.

Shirley's masque presented, with even more elaboration than that of Townshend, the *Triumph of Peace*. But Peace was associated with Law and Justice, as befitted the profession of the young men who presented the masque and took the various parts. In it they sang such pretty compliments as this:

To you, great King and Queen, whose smile
Doth scatter blessings through this isle,
   To make it best
   And wonder of the rest,

> We pay the duty of our birth;
> Proud to wait upon that earth
> Whereon you move,
> Which shall be nam'd—
> And by your chast embraces famed—
> The Paradise of Love.[37]

Shirley's *Triumph of Peace* was followed within a few months by the Shrove Tuesday masque of 1634 at Court, the most ambitious and successful yet given in the royal circle. Thomas Carew's *Coelum Britannicum* carried the glorification of the king and queen to even greater heights, not omitting a spectacular tableau—machinery by Inigo Jones—displaying England, Scotland and Ireland watched over by a protective genius, a 'young man in a white embroidered robe, upon his fair hair an olive garland with wings at his shoulders, and holding in his hand a cornucopia fill'd with corn and fruits'. The theme of the masque was set forth by the god Mercury who thus addressed the king and queen:

> From the high Senate of the gods, to You
> Bright glorious Twins of Love and Majesty,
> Before whose Throne three warlike Nations bend
> Their willing knees, on whose Imperial browes
> The Regall Circle prints no awfull frownes
> To fright your Subjects, but whose calmer eyes
> Shed joy and safety on their melting hearts
> That flow with cheerfull loyall reverence....

Two years before Carew had described the king's subjects as 'obdurate'; by 1634 he had accepted the easy Court view that they were cheerful, loyal and reverent. He, or rather Mercury using his words, next commended the virtues of the royal pair:

> Your exemplar life
> Hath not alone transfus'd a zealous heat
> Of imitation through your vertuous Court
> By whose bright blaze your Pallace is become
> The envied patterne of the underworld,
> But the aspiring flame hath kindled heaven;
> Th' immortall bosomes burne with emulous fires,
> *Jove* rivalls your great vertues, Royall Sir,
> And *Juno*, Madam, your attractive graces....

Moved by the virtues of Charles and his queen, Jove has decided to lead a reformed life and remove from the skies the numerous mistresses whom he had pensioned off by placing them there as stars. But what new stars is he to set up instead? Addressing the king, Mercury goes on:

> In whose vacant roomes
> First you succeed, and of the wheeling Orbe
> In the most eminent and conspicuous point,
> With dazeling beames, and spreading magnitude,
> Shine the bright Pole-starre of this Hemispheare.
> Next, by your side, in a triumphant Chaire,
> And crown'd with *Ariadnes* Diadem,
> Sits the fair consort of your heart, and Throne....

and later:

> Then shall you see
> The sacred hand of bright Eternitie
> Mould you to Stars, and fix you in the Spheare.[38]

The idea of a virtuous and fruitful royal family at the centre of the peaceful and prosperous kingdoms

was, during the middle 1630's, an important part of
the conventional picture which Court poets and
others favourable to the Court were glad to propagate. As a picture it has charm. If the serious
matter of government had been in capable hands,
this idea of the chaste, virtuous and happy Court
might have done something to make the royal family
popular. But as a substitute for effective government it was useless. The idea was praised very
prettily in the occasional verses of Thomas Pestel
who celebrated his appointment as chaplain to
Queen Henrietta Maria by a stream of poems in
praise of King Carolus and Queen Maria rather
thinly disguised as Locarus and Amira, and em-
bellished with some excursions into elementary
French. King Locarus he described as:

> a King as chast as faire,
> Whose only blisse Enthroned is
> En nostre-Dame de Medicis.

Over Queen Henrietta Maria—Amira—Nostre
Dame de Medicis, he was ecstatic beyond the
frontiers of idolatry:

> You forraigne princes that will vowe
> A Pilgrimage of Fame-a
> Come make your offrings here and bowe
> Your heads to Nostre Dame-a.
> If moderne Ladies sick doe fall
> Of Pride, or Ignorance-a,
> Come hither and be curéd all
> With fleure d'elice of France-a.

> And you (Sweet Charles) the sole delight
> And ioye of all mankynd-a
> In Robes and sevrall crounes so bright
> Can no such Jewell find-a,
> She was ordaind, for such a king
> That equall Virtues had-a,
> Which makes both Court and Countrie sing
> With hearts that be full glad-a.

In another poem on the king he declared:

> Our foes admire without all noyse
> How he preservs our peace
> And westerne world cann contrepoyse
> Make wealth and arts encrease,
> With Forts of wood, on walls of flood
> Maynteyning all true British blood:
> While his Soule, do'es guide the whole
> Religion of the Northerne Pole.[39]

Whatever he may have meant by the religion of the Northern Pole, Pestel was quite explicitly acclaiming the king's policy of the year 1636, with his line on 'forts of wood, on walls of flood'. Though he had abandoned any coherent or active foreign policy the king had never lost his genuine interest in the navy. This is not the place to describe the notorious difficulties that he encountered when he tried to raise, through Ship-money, the necessary funds for the extension of the fleet for the defence of the English coasts from piracy and of English fisheries and territorial waters from trespassers. Prominent in his building programme was the great ship, the largest to have been built in England, the *Sovereign of*

the Seas. The name originally suggested for her,
and indicated by her figure-head, was the *Edgar*.[40]
King Edgar, the Anglo-Saxon monarch who was
said to have been rowed in his barge by six—or
according to some authorities, by eight—tributary
kings, was rather a favourite with King Charles I,
possibly because he was traditionally known as
'Edgar the Peaceful' and had been, if the chroniclers
spoke true, a small, slight and beautiful person.

The king had a propagandist purpose in the building of the *Sovereign*. The naval programme was
partly intended to stop criticism of his cautious
foreign policy, which had become vocal again with
the catastrophic decline of the Protestant cause in
Europe. The death of the King of Sweden had been
followed by the shattering defeat of the Protestant
forces at Nördlingen in 1634. By the middle thirties
the Spanish–Austrian fortunes were again in the ascendant, and the fears of English Protestants were acute.

A little popular enthusiasm for the new ship was
stimulated by ballads and pamphlets; but not as
much as there would have been if the king had
combined naval expansion with the abandonment of
neutrality in Europe. As a subject of general con-
versation the king's new ship was shortly and entirely stifled by the hubbub of interest in the rights
and wrongs of Hampden's Ship-money case.

Thus, for compliments on his naval strength, the
king had to depend on courtier poets. Edmund

Waller came in with a finely wrought piece of adulation:

> Where'er thy navy spreads her canvas wings,
> Homage to thee, and peace to all she brings;
> The French and Spaniard, when thy flags appear,
> Forget their hatred, and consent to fear....
> Ships heretofore in seas like fishes sped,
> The mighty still upon the smaller fed;
> Thou on the deep imposest nobler laws,
> And by that justice hast removed the cause
> Of those rude tempests, which, for rapine sent,
> Too oft, alas! involved the innocent.
> Now shall the Ocean, as thy Thames, be free
> From both those fates, of storms and piracy....
> Should nature's self invade the world again
> And o'er the centre spread the liquid main,
> Thy power were safe, and her destructive hand
> Would but enlarge the bounds of thy command;
> Thy dreadful fleet would style thee lord of all,
> And ride in triumph o'er the drownéd ball.[41]

In the following year there was talk of a naval expedition to Madagascar to be led by the king's seventeen-year-old nephew Prince Rupert. The wild scheme came to nothing, but this did not prevent William Davenant from writing an heroic poem on the subject describing the conquest of the island and the establishment of the prince's government there. To this flight of fancy Sir John Suckling, who always had a refreshing vein of common sense, responded in the following terms:

> What princes poets are! those things
> The great ones stick at, and our very Kings

Lay down, they venture on; and with great ease
Discover, conquer what and where they please.
Some phlegmatic sea captain would have staid
For money now, or victuals; not have weighed
Anchor without 'em; thou (Will) dost not stay
So much as for a wind, but go'st away,
Land'st, view'st the country; fight'st, put'st all to rout
Before another could be putting out.
And now the news in town is, Davenant's come
From Madagascar fraught with laurel home;
And welcome Will, for the first time; but prithee
In thy next voyage bring the gold too with thee.[42]

It would have been fortunate for the king if more of
the now plentiful population of poets at his cultured
Court had written in this satirical vein and so done
something to dispel the dangerous illusions in which
he increasingly lived. But to the royal ear praise
alone was welcome; it was a weakness on which his
more active and intelligent ministers, Laud and
Wentworth, commented with anxiety. Court poetry
continued to minister to his self-deception and there
would have been no corrective from the popular
ballad poetry of the 1630's, even had he listened to
it, for it had become cautious in political comment.
The censorship which the king imposed on the
printed opinions of his subjects by means of the Star
Chamber had had its effect. Ballads with open or
implied political comment vanished, and the ballad
writers concentrated on such safe and universally
popular subjects as young people crossed in love and
horrid murders.

But the anxieties which shadowed this supposedly halcyon time can be detected now and again in the work of more thoughtful poets. George Herbert even before he died in 1633 had written that prophetic anxious line:

> Religion stands on tiptoe in our land
> Ready to pass to the American strand.

Other passages in his writings reveal his disquiet at the 'debates and fretting jealousies' at work within the Church. The same anxiety is often to be found in the earlier poems of William Cartwright, the Oxford divine, and of Richard Crashaw, at Cambridge. The intellectuals, unlike the courtiers, could not fail to be aware of the bitterness of religious disagreement in the country and the dangers to peace and order which this involved. Men who wrote with serenity of spirit from inside the Anglican fold were apt to emphasise the threat from outside, the distractions and dangers of schism. Others perceived the dangers that arose from within, from the corruptions and inadequacies that made the Church vulnerable to criticism. While Archbishop Laud struck at the external dangers to the Church, by interfering with conventicles and private religious gatherings and by silencing Puritan preachers, he could, for evident economic reasons, do little to reduce the evil of pluralism or to solve the incessant problems over tithes. These provoked critics of the Church, who might later develop into ferocious enemies. Brooding on pluralists, Milton could not keep them out of his elegy on Edward King:

> How well could I have spared for thee young swain
> Enow of such as for their bellies' sake
> Creep and intrude and climb into the fold?
> Of other care they little reckoning make
> Than how to scramble at the shearers' feast
> And shove away the worthy bidden guest—

King Charles would not have been willing to recognise the truth in Milton's bitter lines; the atmosphere of praise and compliment in which he and his queen lived had induced in him an unwillingness to believe that he, or the institutions of Church and State as he guided them, had in any serious degree fallen short of his ideals.

He was taken by surprise when rebellion broke out in Scotland in 1638 against the very beautiful Prayer Book which he wished to impose on his subjects there. He never understood their objections to it. His first attempt to subdue the Scots by force of arms was a failure; faced by an army much larger than any he had managed to raise from his very unwilling English subjects he bought peace by concessions at the Pacification at Berwick. This truce was celebrated by Abraham Cowley in a poem of courtly compliment:

> Welcome, great Sir, with all the joy that's due
> To the return of *Peace* and *You*,
> Two greatest *Blessings* which this age can know;
> For *that* to *Thee*, for *Thee* to Heav'n we ow.

> Others by *War* their *Conquests* gain,
> You like a *God* your ends obtain.
> Who when rude *Chaos* for his help did call,
> Spoke but the *Word* and sweetly *Order'd* all....

So far the compliment, but in the closing verse
Cowley writes:

> This noise at home was but *Fates* policie
> To raise our Spirits more high.
> So a bold *Lyon* ere he seeks his prey,
> Lashes his sides, and roars, and then away.
> How would the *German Eagle* fear,
> To see a new *Gustavus* there?[43]

This most devoted Royalist is evidently suggesting
that the king will follow his expedition to Scotland
by at last intervening for the Protestant cause and
entering Germany as a new Gustavus, a successor to
the glorious king of Sweden. The lines are particularly interesting because they reflect a temporary but very widespread belief. It was rumoured
that Charles had recognised, in the revolt of his
Scottish subjects, the death-warrant of his pacific
policy in Europe, that he had recognised the power
of Protestant sentiment in his dominions and would,
perhaps at the head of that very Scottish army which
had defied him, enter the European conflict to take
over the part of Protestant champion left vacant by
the king of Sweden eight years before. This rumour
for a few weeks caused a flutter of diplomatic speculation on the continent. Soon, however, it became
clear that, so far from leading his Scottish subjects

to fight in Germany, the king intended to raise a new army against them at home, to repudiate the terms which had been forced from him, and—if necessary with the help of a gigantic loan from Spain—to extinguish the puritan-Protestant opposition alike in Scotland and England.

At this juncture an event occurred which caused several of the popular ballad writers to raise loud if rather uncertain voices. A Spanish fleet carrying troops to the Netherlands took refuge from the Dutch in the Downs where on 11 October 1639 it was attacked and almost entirely destroyed by the Dutch under Admiral Tromp. This new Spanish Tragedy, as the ballad writer, Laurence Price, called it,[44] inspired about half a dozen ballads, but their writers did not celebrate the event as whole-heartedly as they would have done thirty years earlier. Their sympathies were on the whole with the Dutch, but they were cautious about uttering any opinion about the rights and wrongs of the matter and did not jubilate over the shattered Spaniards. This attitude in part reflected a growing hostility to the Dutch who, from being Protestants in distress, were now becoming competitors in trade. But it also reflected the anxiety of the ballad writers not to offend the Court, and some considerable doubt as to which side the Court was on. Whether the king was for or against the Spaniards, it was in any case an embarrassing comment on his

boast to be ruler of the sea that the Dutch had fought
the battle in English territorial waters, and in utter
disregard of the English fleet. The situation was
thoroughly confused and no one can blame the
ballad writers for winding up their accounts of the
great Battle of the Downs with sentiments like this:

> God bless our gracious King and Queen
> And our brave English fleet
> And give them victory on the seas
> When they with foes do meet,
> Defend them from ill sands and rocks
> And lord their battle fight
> As thou didst for Elisabeth
> In the year 88.

The king meanwhile made ready for a second war
on the Scots. At Court the illusion that he would
easily overcome his enemies was stimulated by the
courtly compliments usual at Christmas and New
Year. Davenant surpassed himself in the words that
he composed for the Twelfth Night masque, the last
in which the king was personally to appear. Charles
impersonated the wise ruler Philogenes, the lover of
his people, who, breaking from a cloud, subdued
faction and civil strife, and provoked a song of
praise from his admiring subjects:

> All that are harsh, all that are rude,
> Are by your harmony subdued;
> Yet so into obedience wrought,
> As if not forced to it, but taught.
> Live still, the pleasure of our sight;
> Both our examples and delight....[45]

Once again the poet called up the enchanted illusion that a cultivated and virtuous king would exorcise all the dangers in the State. The illusion is echoed again in lines written a few months later by Richard Crashaw to celebrate the birth of the king's youngest son, Prince Henry. After celebrating the children already born to the royal pair Crashaw goes on:

> More Princes come:
> Rebellion, stand thou by; Mischief, make room:
> War, Bloud and Death (Names all averse from Ioy)
> Heare this, We have another bright-ey'd Boy:
> That word's a warrant, by whose vertue I
> Have full authority to bid you Dy....
> But thou, sweet supernumerary Starre,
> Shine forth; nor fear the threats of boyst'rous Warre.
> The face of things has therefore frown'd a while
> On purpose, that to thee and thy pure smile
> The world might ow an universall calm....[46]

Such lines could be dismissed as empty pieces of decoration, graceful garlands for a royal cradle, with no real significance; but there is evidence from other sources that the birth of a third son to the queen was really regarded at Court as a happy political omen and did something to increase the feckless optimism with which the king hastened towards a second war with his Scottish subjects.

In the spring of this year 1640 Parliament met after a ten-year interval, and Martin Parker the ballad-monger came out with a series of verses that reflected the popular view of the occasion. A genuine loyalty to the king is coupled with an equally genuine hope that the calling of Parliament will solve all problems:

> Come the merriest of the nine,
> And now unto my aid incline,
> I need a little helpe of thine
> For now I have intent
> Unto the world to say and sing
> The praises of our royall King,
> Who now, this present hopefull Spring
> Hath called a Parliament.
>
> This happy Aprill will, I trust,
> Give all true subjects reason just
> Of joy to feele a pleasant gust,
> To yeeld them hearts content:
> For we may be assur'd by this,
> If anything hath been amisse,
> Our King and State will all redresse
> In this good Parliament.

The king, when in the thirteenth verse Parker ultimately reaches him, is 'our gracious King, our Charles the Great, our joy's sweet complement'.[47]

Martin Parker's hopes like those of many another were dashed by the failure of king and Parliament to come to any agreement. Meanwhile the king, in the teeth of what was now almost nation-wide obstruction, went on with his preparations against the Scots, recalling Strafford his man of iron from Ireland to assist him.

In the summer and autumn of 1640 the be-

wildered London ballad writers were a prey to a
conflict of interests. There was, for obvious reasons,
no love lost between ballad writers and Puritans. In
a fight between the king and the Presbyterian Scots,
the overriding sympathies of the average ballad
writer were therefore likely to be with the king.
But the ballad writer also depended for his success
on reflecting the opinions of his public, and the
majority of London citizens, exasperated by the
policies of the Crown, by the inept and privileged
interference of courtiers in trade and manufacture,
and by the king's quarrel with Parliament, were by
now convinced that the king was not so much anti-
Puritan as pro-Popish, and were bitterly opposed to
the Scots war. Martin Parker and one or two others
made valiant efforts to stimulate enthusiasm for the
war on Scotland thus:

> It much importeth Englands honour
> Such faithless Rebels to oppose,
> And elevate Saint Georges banner,
> Against them as our countries foes,
> and they shall see,
> how stoutly we,
> (for Royall *Charles* with courage free)
> will fight if there occasion be.[48]

The majority of the English thought that there
was no occasion to fight. Indeed they were more
than ready to respond to a different kind of appeal
coming from the other side of the border. A Scots

ballad writer addressed to them these lines, reminiscent in rhythm of a metrical psalm:

> You gallant English spirits lay this to heart
> And with the Lord against his foes take part;...
> Join hearts and hands with Leslies thund'ring band,
> To chase these Romish locusts from your land.[49]

The defeat of the king's half-hearted forces at
Newburn—that 'infamous irreparable rout'—was
only to be expected; but Charles was still unwilling
to believe that the fault lay in his policy or the unwillingness of his soldiers to fight. His courtiers
clung to the belief that Scottish intrigue had undermined his friends and corrupted his followers—a
point of view which the courtier Davenant was to
propagate in his poem *The Plots*:

> We fear'd not the *Scots* from the High-land, nor Low-land;
> Though some of their Leaders did craftily brave us,
> With boasting long Service in *Russe* and in *Poland*,
> And with their fierce breeding under *Gustavus*.
>
> Not the Tales of their Combats more strange than Romances,
> Nor *Sandy's* screw'd Cannon did strike us with wonder;
> Nor their Kettle-Drums sounding before their long Launces;
> But *Scottish* Court-whispers struck surer than Thunder....[50]

It was a face-saving excuse. The truth was that no
war could be fought when the majority in England
was against it. A popular English ballad, written
shortly after the conclusion of hostilities, with its
refrain *Gramercy good Scot*, reflected the general
relief of the king's subjects in the south because the

Scots invasion had compelled him to call Parliament and had temporarily overthrown his government. Two verses of it sum up with unusual precision the chief reasons for the dislike of the royal government, the king's attempts to make money by granting monopolies, under the thin disguise of patents, and his persistent pro-Spanish foreign policy:

Oh how high were they flown with their floorishing hope,
With their patents for pins, tobacco and sope,
False dice and false cards, besides the great fyne
They yearly receiv'd by enhancing of wine,
The tide is now turn'd, let us drink th' other pot,
And merrily sing, *gramercy good Scot.*

Although this fair island abound with foule crimes,
The Parliament saith, we shall see better times,
Then let us not faint as men without hope,
An halter for traitors, an hemp for the Pope,
Let Spain and the Strumpet of Babylon plot,
Yet we shall be safe, *gramercy good Scot.*[51]

The same idea was more ponderously expressed in a ballad printed a few months later in praise of the Long Parliament. In this the king's subjects deplore the halcyon days which the court poets had celebrated in a different strain:

Like silly Sheepe they did us daily sheare,
Like Asses strong our backes were made to beare,
Intollerable burdens, year by year,
No hope, no help, no comfort did appeare,
But from the great Counsell of the King,
And the Kings great Counsell.

With taxes, and Monopolies opprest,
Ship-money, Souldiers, Knighthood, and the rest,
The Coate and Conduct-money was no jest,
Then think good neighbours how much we are blest
In the great Counsell of the King,
And the King's great Counsell.

Were not these plagues worse than a sweeping rot,
Oh how unkindly did they use the *Scot*;
But those bould blades did prove so fiery hot,
This swinging Bowle to them, this other Pot
To the great Counsell of the King,
And the King's great Counsell.[52]

The moment of blissful illusions was over.
Strafford was arrested soon after the Long Parliament met, tried in April and executed in May 1641,
a subject which fired the fancy of poets from the
best to the worst. Popular ballads were hostile but
dignified; the drama of the great minister's fall, and
the shocking spectacle of the king relinquishing to
his death a man whose only fault had been his single-
minded support of the Crown made a deep impression. The somewhat tame muse of Sir John
Denham was stirred by the tragedy, and if his opening couplet is commonplace, it sums up the general
feeling that, for Strafford's friends as well as for his
enemies, the last act crowned the play:

Great *Strafford!* worthy of that Name, though all
Of thee could be forgotten, but thy fall,
Crusht by Imaginary Treasons weight,
Which too much Merit did accumulate:

64

As Chymists Gold from Brass by fire would draw,
Pretexts are into Treason forg'd by Law.
His Wisdom such, at once it did appear
Three Kingdoms wonder, and three Kingdoms fear;...
Such was his force of Eloquence, to make
The Hearers more concern'd than he that spake;
Each seem'd to act that part, he came to see,
And none was more a looker on than he:
So did he move our passion, some were known
To wish for the defence, the Crime their own.
Now private pity strove with publick hate,
Reason with Rage, and Eloquence with Fate;
Now they could him, if he could them forgive;
He's not too guilty, but too wise to live....[53]

Denham had watched the trial and wrote from knowledge; the last two lines, from the Royalist point of view, summed up what lay behind the determination of the king's opponents to have Strafford's head.

Fanshawe in describing the trial which he also witnessed was not quite so happy, but the impression is the same. Of Strafford's defence he wrote:

Times shall admiring read it, and *this age*,
Though now it *hisse*, claps when he leaves the Stage;
So *stand* or *fall*, none *stood* so, or so *fell*;
This farre-famed Tryall hath no paralell....[54]

Fanshawe made the tragic point that it was Strafford's letter releasing the king from the promise he had given to save his life which led to the signing of his death-warrant; thus Strafford destroyed himself by turning 'against himself his conquering eloquence'. But the most striking summary of the tragedy, which was also a prophecy of worse to come, appeared in a brief anonymous broadsheet after the execution:

> Here lies wise and valiant dust
> Huddled up 'twixt fit and just;
> Strafford, who was hurried hence
> 'Twixt treason and convenience.
> He spent his time here in a mist;
> A Papist, yet a Calvinist;
> His Prince's nearest joy and grief
> He had, yet wanted all relief;
> The prop and ruin of the State;
> The People's violent love and hate;
> One in extremes loved and abhorred.
> Riddles lie here, or in a word,
> Here lies blood; and let it lie
> Speechless still and never cry.[55]

Within a few years these lines were ascribed to John Cleveland, who by the later 1640's had become the most famous writer of political satires in England. The ascription has been challenged, but I am inclined to think it correct. For one thing the writer knows that Strafford was a Calvinist. Now it is a paradoxical fact that this friend of Archbishop Laud and principal prop of King Charles's government was inclined to Calvinism in his personal religion. But this was not at all widely known, as Strafford kept his religion very much to himself. The populace no doubt ignorantly called him 'Papist' because he had strongly supported the king's pro-Spanish foreign policy, and he had even tried to re-float the foundering government on a huge loan from Spain. The irony of calling this Calvinist a Papist would have struck most forcibly someone who knew the great minister's personal religious views, and Cleveland, who was a Fellow of St John's College, Cambridge, where Strafford had been educated, may easily have picked up this odd piece of information from some of the older Fellows of his College.

With this broadsheet we seem to enter a new era. The shocked and startled followers of the Court no less than the ballad and broadsheet writers were now seriously engaged in the events they described. Yet it was not to be altogether the end of make-believe. The time for pleasing allegory had passed, but the atmosphere it had left behind could not so easily be dispelled and the Royalist poets, far into the harsh years of the war, still from time to time ministered to the belief in a gracious and in some sense god-like king whose clouded visage must ultimately shine forth again in all its splendour. The illusion stayed with the king himself longer than anyone.

During the trial of Strafford, the king, clutching at the rather tenuous hope of a rich alliance as a means of saving the Crown, had arranged the marriage of his eldest daughter to the Prince of Orange's only son. The marriage took place on the eve of Strafford's execution, and against the background of an anxious and harassed Court the child

bride went to the altar with a host of pretty atten-
dants all in cloth of silver. This incident William
Cartwright set into poetry:

> Amids such Heat of Business, such State throng
> Disputing Right and Wrong
> And the sour Justle of Unclosed Affairs
> What mean those Glorious Pairs?
> That Youth? that Virgin? those all dresst?
> The Whole, and every Face, a Feast?
> Great omen! o ye Powers
> May this your Knot, be ours.
> Thus while cold things with hot did jar,
> And dry with moist made mutual war,
> Love from that Mass did leap;
> And what was but an heap
> Rude and ungathered, swift as thought was hurled
> Into the Beauty of an Ordered World.[56]

Dryden was to echo the lovely lines and enhance
their beauty fifty years later in the second of his
Hymns for Saint Cecilia's Day. But this most
luminous poem sprang from a very dark hour.

The situation moved with alarming rapidity towards the final breach between king and Parliament,
its course marked out by popular ballads of a jovial
brutality. The abolition by Parliament of the Court
of Star Chamber had set the press free—a development which Parliament had not quite bargained for,
but against which they took no steps as long as
majority opinion was on their side. As the king's
friends fled the country, a popular ballad made fun
of their 'running disease' to the refrain of:

Keep thy head on thy shoulders
And I will keep mine.

Though Wentworths beheaded,
Should any Repyne,
Thers others may come
To the Blocke beside he:
Keep thy head on thy Shoulders
And I will keep mine;
For what is all this to thee or to mee?
Then merrily and cheerily
Lets drink off our Beere,
Let who as will run for it
Wee will stay here.[57]

The arrest of the Bishops, late in December 1641, for protesting against mob rule at Westminster brought this:

Come down Prelates, all arow,
Your Protestation brings you low,
Have we not alwayes told you so;
You are too sawcy Prelates,
Come downe Prelates.

Yorke, when you were *Lincolne* of late,
You were in the *Tower*, yet still you will prate,
How dare you Protest against the whole State,
You are too bold *Yorke*,
Come down proud *Yorke*.

And so on through all the bishops until the happy conclusion:

They were sent to the Tower, as the old yeer ended,
By a dozen together,
In frosty weather.[58]

A fortnight later the king fled from the capital and both sides began to prepare for war. Occasionally out of the heart of much disturbed London the voices of the king's plebeian friends—he had some—were raised. Martin Parker seems to have been temporarily at a loss, but John Taylor the ex-Thames lighterman and self-styled 'Water Poet' was always voluble. On the eve of the Civil War he preached a melancholy good sense:

> They are most blind, with ignorance besotted
> Who think war's councel in a chamber plotted,
> Must so be acted with the dint of sword
> As it was wisely talked of at the board.
> Methinks the proverb should not be forgot
> That wars are sweet, to those that know them not.[59]

But the situation was beyond the reach of argument; the blessed 1630's when the Court and king were lulled in false peace were as if they had never been, and, in the rare strong phrase from Sir William Davenant, grown serious at last, 'in Westminster storms Whitehall went to wrack'.[60]

III

POETS AT WAR

So far I have considered two different kinds of political comment by the poets: the verses of the sophisticated poets who, in the personal rule of King Charles I, with few exceptions, took their inspiration from the Court, and the ballads of the popular writers who aimed to please a more humble public whose tastes and preoccupations they shared. In the Civil War the frontier between the two kinds of comment became blurred. The supporters of each side in the political struggle recognised the need for propaganda that would strike home quickly to men's minds. Under the stress of events a new, simpler and more explicit kind of writing became general.

This development is extremely noticeable in prose, where the change from the complex and mannered writing usual in the earlier part of the century to the brisk and forthright manner of newspapers, pamphlets and public statements in the Civil War is very striking. In the same way Puritan preachers, who aimed at a wide and simple rather than a select and educated audience, had developed a strong and dramatic manner of argument, in contrast to the sophisticated subtlety of the famous

Anglican preachers. The influence of popular preachers and of the now rapidly developing breed of journalists on prose can hardly be over-estimated: these writers whatever their own educational equipment, and some were very well educated, perceived that the first essential was to communicate, effectively and quickly, whether they were imparting ideas or doctrine or facts.

With the breakdown of censorship in 1641—it was several years before it was reimposed—official and free lance propagandists of all parties and all views leapt into print. News and comment were regularly published and eagerly bought. The development was deplored by many writers who themselves took advantage of it; it was invariably the other man, or the other side, whom they wished to silence. Thus George Wither, one of the most prolific pamphleteers and poets on the Parliamentary side, angrily complained of the use that his Royalist compeers were making of the printing press:

> For it is now imploy'd by Paper-wasters,
> By mercenary soules, and Poetasters,
> Who weekly utter slanders, libells, lies,
> Under the name of specious novelties.

To satisfy his rage he imagines a group of these writers on trial in Parnassus, before a jury of twelve poets; he himself is the foreman and Shakespeare brings up the rear. The charge is that they are mercenary scribblers who

...For wicked ends
Had the *Castalian Spring* defil'd with gall;
And chang'd by witchcraft, most Satyricall,
The bayes of *Helicon*, and myrtles mild,
To pricking hauthornes, and to hollyes wild...;

worse still, they

added fewell to the direfull flame
Of civill discord, and domesticke blowes,
By the incentives of malicious prose.[61]

Wither's cry of rage expresses very neatly what
was happening to verse as well as prose. The myrtles
and the bays can be taken to stand for the subtle and
cultivated conceits of earlier Caroline poetry, phrases
and fashions transplanted from foreign soil and
acclimatised in the English garden; the hawthorns
and hollies stand for the native hedgerow product,
the popular ballads and simple rhymes which were
more commonly used in the Civil War.

From the outbreak of the war even some poets
who were highly skilled in the fashionable manner
of the 1630's adopted a simple, even a crude, form
of writing when their intention was to defend a
cause—usually the king's—to as wide a public as
possible. Along with this simplification went the
rapid development of satire, sometimes closely
allied with the popular ballad. Much of this political
propaganda is awkward, much is genuinely comic,
some is really witty and a little of it is impressive in
its skill. It is the dawn chorus of that great age of

political satire which was to follow later in the century. Among this hurried wartime balladry are the sources of Samuel Butler, whose *Hudibras*, the greatest of the satires on the Puritans, appeared only after the Restoration; here, too, are the forerunners of the transcendent Dryden.

Such developments meant death to the elegance and delicacy of the previous decade, though grace and courtliness did not immediately vanish. To the ears of an older generation such music was still welcome, perhaps especially welcome above the strident noise of war. There had to be moments of escape, reversions now and again among the king's followers to a manner more suited to the orderly peace of Whitehall than the disorderly din of wartime Oxford, where soldiers slept on the ground under canvas slung across the narrow streets, and the wives and daughters of the courtiers lay two or three in a bed in poky rooms over tradesmen's shops.

These younger sisters to the Altheas and Sacharissas, Celias and Corinnas of the preceding decade helped to carry on a little longer the tradition of poesy and gallantry. Aubrey has described Lady Isabella Thynne coming into the gardens of Trinity College 'with a theorbo or lute played before her', and how she and 'fine Mrs Fanshawe her great and intimate friend was wont to come to our chapel mornings half dressed, like angels'; and once unwisely they attempted a frolic with old Dr Kettle, the President of the College, who quickly sent the wild, pretty young things about their business.[62] On another occasion the Parliamentary soldiers, having intercepted some letters from the king's quarters, were disgusted to find in them, when they broke the seals, no valuable information, nothing but some pretty love gossip signed Amorella and Diaphenia.[63]

So too, in spite of the movement towards a fierce or humorous clarity of statement, there was still now and again a daring image, a highly metaphysical conceit in this wartime poetry. On the king's escape disguised as a serving man, John Cleveland could still write:

> O the accursed stenography of fate!
> Our princely eagle shrunk into a bat![64]

which in intellectual daring, not to say showing off, is as far from the simplicity of ballad diction as it can well be. Vaughan's phrase on the same subject—'our hieroglyphic King'[65]—is nearly as striking. The stream of courtly verse runs for a little longer before it goes underground, to return in a different form with the peace of the Protectorate and to enjoy a shallow revival at the Restoration. So Robert Herrick, whose lyrical art was not attuned to war, welcomed the advance of the king into the west country in the summer of 1644 with this:

> Welcome, most welcome to our vows and us,
> Most great and universal Genius.

> The Drooping West which hitherto has stood
> As one in long-lamented widowhood,
> Looks like a Bride now, or a bed of flowers
> Newly refresht both by the sun and showers.
> War which before was horrid now appears
> Lovely in you, brave Prince of Cavaliers.
> A deal of courage in each bosom springs
> By your access, o you the best of Kings,
> Ride on with all white Omens, so that where
> Your Standard's up, we fix a Conquest there.[66]

This delightful piece of loyal enthusiasm did not wholly represent the feelings of the west, for very few recruits joined the king's standard on this occasion. The palm goes to Abraham Cowley for carrying the masque spirit into this troubled time. When the queen, after going abroad to raise money and arms, rejoined her husband in the summer of 1643, they met formally on Edgehill, not quite a year after the battle had been fought there. Describing this incident, Cowley suggested some necessary fumigation of the site to make it ready for the glad occasion:

> Through the Glad vail, Ten thousand *Cupids* fled
> And Chas'd the wandring spirits of *Rebels* dead,
> Still the lewd scent of Powder did they fear,
> And scatter'd *Eastern Smells* through all the Air.... [67]

At this time the royal victory seemed not only possible but imminent and the poetic welcome accorded to the queen at Oxford, in the form of a slender volume to which all the university wits contributed, reflects this happy and triumphant mood.

It also contains some very beautiful things. Cartwright, who two years before had written so prettily on the marriage of the king's daughter, celebrated the queen's return in what is perhaps his best poem:

Hallow the Threshold, Crown the Posts anew
The day shall have its due:
Twist all our Victories into one bright wreath
On which let Honour breath,
Then throw it round the Temples of our Queen
Tis She that must preserve those glories green.

When greater Tempests than on Sea before
Received Her on the shore
When She was shot at, for the King's own good,
By Villains hired to Blood,
How bravely did She do, how bravely bear
And show'd though they durst rage, She durst not fear.

Courage was cast about Her like a Dress,
Of solemn Comeliness,
A gather'd Mind and an untroubled Face,
Did give Her dangers grace.
Thus armed with Innocence secure they move
Whose Highest Treason is but Highest Love.[68]

Cartwright was in the very thick of affairs now, as he had hardly been when he wrote the graceful piece on Princess Mary's marriage. I do not think it is simply a historian's reaction to suggest that his greater knowledge of events and his genuine concern for the king's cause make this a much stronger and more satisfying poem than his exquisitely pretty but empty tribute to the princess. In this later poem the flow of sound is accompanied by a flow of

meaning, wrapped in compliments, it is true, and not
perhaps immediately comprehensible to the modern
ear, but none the less genuine meaning, only a little
exaggerated.

> Twist all our victories into one bright wreath...

—in the summer of 1643 there was nothing false in
that line; the Royalists had won a series of splendid
victories ending with the annihilation of Sir William
Waller's force at Roundway Down in the very week
that the queen entered Oxford.

> When greater tempests than on sea before
> Received her on the shore.

The queen had crossed from the Netherlands in
very stormy weather, and on landing at Bridlington
had been bombarded by ships of the Parliamentary
fleet.
> Shot at, for the King's own good
> By villains hired to blood

is a sidelong taunt at the claim, at this time always
made in official Parliamentary statements, that they
were fighting to rescue the king from the evil coun-
sellors who had misled him into war. The praise of
the queen's courage is, on this occasion, no more
than just; and the lovely last line—'Whose Highest
Treason is but Highest Love'—is a reference to her
recent impeachment for treason by Parliament.

The theme of the queen's impeachment was taken
up by another poet whose verses appear in the same
collection. He combines it very ingeniously, by a

deft use of double meaning, with her bringing of supplies and ammunition for the king. His name was W. Barker and nothing else of his seems to be known.

> Shine forth with doubled light that rebels may
> Or sleep in darkness or else see 'tis day;
> And treason stoop, forced by commanding charms
> Either to kiss your hand, or fear your arms.[69]

Cleveland, the most dexterous poet to deal in political verse, in a poem on Prince Rupert used the heightened classical allusions so common in the elegant poems of the 1630's. But this time, provided we take the lines, as Cleveland certainly meant them to be taken, with a certain humour, his classical comparison is not (as with Carew or Townshend) merely ornamental; it is lavishly flattering, but also ingeniously apt. Cleveland was describing the notorious daring of the prince and his almost equally notorious good luck: though he was always in the hottest of the battle, he had never yet been wounded. Cleveland therefore compared him to Perseus, son of Danae, begotten by Jupiter in a shower of gold:

> He gags their guns, defeats their dire intent;
> The cannons do but lisp and compliment.
> Sure, Jove descended in a leaden shower
> To get this Perseus; hence the fatal power
> Of shot is strangled. Bullets thus allied
> Fear to commit an act of parricide.[70]

More seriously, William Cartwright, in his elegy
on Sir Bevil Grenville killed at the battle of Lans-
down, made a resolute and not unsuccessful effort
to translate into the conventions of verse a detailed
description of a deed of great valour. Grenville,
leading his Cornish pikemen, had forced his way up
a steep bluff under heavy fire, and had taken and
held a position on very difficult ground against no
less than four cavalry charges. 'They stood as upon
the eaves of an house for steepness but as unmovable
as a rock', wrote one eye-witness. The poem gains a
good deal from the double meaning, skilfully ex-
ploited, of the word *stand*: the *stand* that Grenville
and his men made on the top of the ridge, and the
fact that the formation Grenville led was known as a
stand of pikes:

> When now th'incensed rebel proudly came
> Down like a torrent without bank or dam;
> When undeserved success urged on their force
> That thunder must come down to stop their course
> Or Grenville must step in; Then Grenville stood
> And with Himself opposed and checked the flood....
> His courage worked like flames, cast heat about,
> Here, there, on this, on that side, none gave out;
> Not any pike in that renowned stand
> But took new force from his inspired hand;
> Soldier encouraged soldier, man urged man,
> And he urged all; so much example can.
> Hurt upon hurt, wound upon wound did call,
> He was the but, the mark, the aim of all:
> His soul this while retired from cell to cell,
> At last flew up from all, and then he fell.

But the devoted stand, enraged more
From that his fate, plied hotter than before,
And proud to fall with him, sworn not to yield,
Each sought an honoured grave and gained the field.
Thus, he being fall'n, his action fought anew;
And the dead conquer'd, whiles the living slew.[71]

It is a mannered treatment of a terrible subject and somewhat alien to our taste; this playing with juxtaposition, pun and paradoxes—'the dead conquered while the living slew'—has for us a heartless quality; we cannot quite accept this turning of mortal strife and physical anguish into a literary exercise. But it was acceptable enough to a generation whose ears and minds were attuned to such treatment of a dreadful theme, and who found it moving, even consoling.

A manuscript in the National Library of Scotland, the Memoirs of Richard Augustine Hay, preserves a story which illustrates the way in which a well-turned verse could express, or assuage, even the death agony of the Cavaliers. The incident may serve as an epitaph on the whole Caroline manner. When the Marquis of Montrose was ultimately captured and brought a prisoner into Edinburgh, he was followed on the long, humiliating and weary march from the north by several hundred other captured loyalists. Just as they entered the Tolbooth one of these, a young gentleman of a poetic turn of mind, managed to evade the guard. Approaching his captive commander, he fell upon his knees and recited to him an epigram in verse which he had composed during that terrible march from the lost battle to the inevitable scaffold. The lines, whatever they were, distilled some fragment of beauty, some note of honour, from their common tragedy, and Montrose, the manuscript records, 'his hands being then bound, leaned on his shoulder and wept'.[72]

Death was a very present subject in the years of war, and it was not unusual for poets to use the elegy as a means for praising and propagating their cause. An elegy on Hampden's death after the fight of Chalgrove, from an anonymous London broadsheet, finely described the qualities of the great Parliamentary leader. But the portrait, though it was intended as a personal likeness, also had another purpose, namely to contradict the accusations of self-interest which the Cavaliers, in prose and verse, were successfully putting out against their opponents.

> But—noble soul—his purer thoughts were free
> From all corruption; he not valued friends
> A fair estate nor self propounded ends
> Any preferment, nor ought else above
> A quiet conscience and his nation's love.[73]

Very different was the portrait of Hampden by that vocal Cavalier Abraham Cowley. Cowley noted the fact, which Royalists were quick to read as a stroke of divine justice, that Hampden received

his death-wound at or near the very place where he
had first called the local forces together against the
king, on the outbreak of the war:

> Such fatal vengeance did wronged *Chalgrove* show,
> Where Hampden both began and ended too
> His cursed Rebellion, where his Soul's repaid
> With separation, great as that he made,
> Hampden whose spirit moved o'r this mighty Frame,
> O' th' British Isle, and out this Chaos came.
> Hampden, the man that taught Confusion's Art,
> His Treasons restless and yet noiseless Heart.
> His Active Brain like *Aetna*'s Top appeared,
> Where Treason's forged, yet no noise outward heard....
> 'Twas he that taught the *Zealous Rout* to rise,
> And be his Slaves for some famed Liberties.
> Him for this Black Design, Hell thought most fit,
> Ah! wretched Man, cursed by too good a Wit.[74]

To Cowley also we owe a pleasing satire on the
Puritan, gentler than *Hudibras* was to be, in which
he cleverly linked the tenets of Puritan religion with
their behaviour, or at least their behaviour as the
Royalists saw it, in the war. The news-sheets of both
parties were much inclined to claim all battles for
victories: the battle of Worcester to which Cowley
refers is of course not the famous battle of 1651,
but an early skirmish in the Civil War in which the
Parliamentary forces had been ignominiously routed.
Cowley begins with a comment on the alleged bad
faith of Parliament—

> For you do hate all swearing so that when
> You've sworn an oath, ye break it straight again....

> But oh, your faith is mighty, that hath been
> As true faith ought to be, of things unseen—
> At Worcester, Brentford, and Edgehill we see
> Only by faith y'have got the victory.
> Such is your faith, and some such unseen way
> The public faith at last your debts will pay....[75]

Jokes about the public faith were frequent in the Civil War. Parliament constantly borrowed money 'on the public faith' which meant that there was no guarantee at all of repayment.

Cowley may have polished these poems later as they do not seem to have been in print until after the Restoration, but they probably circulated in manuscript earlier. At any rate he was a more conscientious and careful craftsman than the impetuous spirits who rushed in with songs and satires for immediate use—some of them hurried and careless but with spirit and vigour enough to become instantly popular. They circulated in manuscript, in song, by word of mouth, or in broadsheets, which were printed and freely circulated in London in Parliament's despite.

The printer's name was usually suppressed, and the numerous clandestine presses were difficult to track down. The ballad sellers were from 1644 onwards under threats of fearful penalties from Parliament if they were caught, but they were for the most part too popular and too well protected by their clients. The Londoners, though they had been predominantly against the king in the year pre-

ceding the war, were by no means all for Parliament
when it began. The natural swing of the pendulum
created a large and growing Royalist public for the
ballads, and once a ballad caught on, no prohibition
could stop its being sung. Martin Parker—who had
been ballad writing since James I's time—did his
last and best service to the Stuarts when he launched
on London early in 1643 the song with the famous
refrain: 'When the King enjoys his own again.'
The tune was a traditional and popular one; tune and
words served not only the Cavaliers but later the
Jacobites, and both were heard about the streets of
London for nearly two centuries.

Whatever their weakness in other fields the
Royalists had more talent at their disposal in the
verse and ballad war. Milton used prose for pamphlet-
eering and Marvell did not turn his poetic genius to
political ends until a later time. The tone was set by
the Cavaliers, especially Cleveland, Denham and
Alexander Brome. Owing to the manner in which
these verses were circulated authorship is often uncertain. Cleveland was the name which was most
often attached to anonymous pieces, a tribute to his
reputation as the most deadly and skilful of the
Cavalier satirists. His authentic pieces include a
mock invocation beginning: 'Most gracious, omni-
potent and everlasting Parliament', and a cheerfully
scurrilous piece on the Divines in the Westminster
Assembly. He was the sharpest and most insistently

topical of the Cavaliers. But the songs of the facile, devil-may-care Alexander Brome reflected most clearly from 1640 until after the Restoration the changing moods of the typical Cavalier. He began with vigorous and confident mockery of the Roundheads in the extremely popular song 'The Clean Contrary Way'. The Roundhead Colonel Venn (much mocked by the Royalists because of his humble origin) is supposed to be exhorting his men:

> Fight on brave Souldiers for the Cause,
> Fear not the *Cavaliers*;
> Their threatenings are as senseless as
> Our *jealousies* and *fears*.
> 'Tis you must *perfect* this great work,
> And all *Malignants* slay,
> You must bring back the *King* again
> The clean contrary way.
>
> When *Charles* we've *bankrupt* made like us,
> Of *Crown* and *power* bereft him;
> And all his loyal subjects *slain*,
> And *none* but *Rebels* left him,
> And when we've plundered all the *Land*,
> And *sent* our *Truncks* away;
> We'll make him then a glorious *Prince*,
> The clean contrary way.
>
> 'Tis to preserve his Majesty,
> That we *against* him fight,
> Nor are we ever *beaten* back,
> Because our cause is right;
> At Kineton, Brentford, Plymouth, York,
> And divers places more;

> What victories we *Saints* obtain'd,
> The like ne'r seen before.
> How often we Prince *Rupert* kill'd
> And bravely *won* the day,
> The wicked *Cavaliers* did run
> The clean contrary way.[76]

The mock speech put into the mouth of one of their enemies was a very popular form of attack. What Brome did for Colonel Venn, Denham gaily did for John Hampden. The occasion was the summer of 1643 when, just before Hampden's death, he was straining all his eloquence and diplomatic ability in Parliament and the city to prevent his weaker colleagues from suing for peace. Plague was raging in the Parliamentary army, food was dear in London, things were very bad. Denham naturally assumed that Hampden was pursuing the war entirely for his own ends. He saw him, as Cowley had done, as the engineering brain behind the whole revolt:

> Did I for this take pains to teach
> Our zealous Ignorants to preach,
> And did their lungs inspire,
> Read them their Text, shew'd them their Parts,
> And taught them all their little Arts
> To fling abroad the Fire?
>
> Sometimes to beg, sometimes to threaten,
> And say the Cavaliers are beaten,
> To stroke the People's ears;
> Then straight when Victory grows cheap,
> And will no more advance the heap,
> To raise the price of Fears?

> But Plague and Famine will come in,
> For they and we are neare of kin,
> And cannot go asunder:
> But while the wicked starve, indeed
> The Saints have ready at their need
> God's Providence and Plunder.[77]

Denham also came in with one of the cleverest Cavalier songs, *The Western Wonder*. The Western Wonder was the skirmish on Sourton Down near Okehampton where the Cavaliers under Hopton were surprised and routed at night during a storm by a force of only about a hundred men under a young man called Chudleigh. It was not a very important check, but the Parliamentary news-sheets made a great deal of it. Denham, very sensibly, instead of denying the overthrow of his friends, merely picked up the Parliamentary version of the story and exaggerated it to ridicule:

> Do you not know, not a fortnight agoe,
> How they bragged of a Western wonder?
> When a hundred and ten, slew five thousand men,
> With the help of Lightning and Thunder?
>
> There *Hopton* was slain, again and again,
> Or else my Author did lye;
> With a new *Thanksgiving*, for the dead who are living,
> To God, and his Servant *Chudleigh*.[78]

Denham was immensely high spirited and very good natured. George Wither, the Parliamentary poet, tried to seize his estate which lay behind the Parliament lines; in spite of this, when Wither was taken prisoner and there was some question of trying him for his life for the things he had written against the king, Aubrey tells us 'Sir John Denham went to the King and desired his majesty not to hang him, for that while George Wither lived he should not be the worst poet in England'.[79] The genuine kindness in begging Wither off has to be weighed against the malicious comment on his verse, and certainly some of George Wither's humourless pro-Parliamentary effusions would easily earn him the title of the worst poet in England. In a recruiting poem written in the summer of 1643 he demonstrated with lumbering ineptitude how not to manage those sonorous lists of great names which from time to time other English poets have impressively worked into their lines:

Let valiant Essex, Warwick, Manchester,
Stout Fairfax, Waller, Roberts, Brooke and Gray
—Who forward for the public safety were—
Be crownéd with a never dying bay.
So crowned be Skippon, Meyrick, Stapelton,
With Hampden, Massey, Brereton and Gell:
The English and the Scottish Middleton,
My noble and my valiant Colonel;
Remembered be with an heroic fame
Balfour and Ramsay, Cromwell and D'Albier,
The Meldrums, and he chiefly of that name
Whose worth did in relieving Hull appear—
Let mentioned be with honourable men
Much daring Luke, and Haslerig the bold,
Aldridge, Brown, Barclay, Holborn, Harvey, Venn,
Brooke, Norton, Springer, Morley, Moore and Gould....[80]

'Much daring Luke' is generally thought to have been the original of Samuel Butler's cowardly fat knight Hudibras, and 'Haslerig the bold' is alleged (but perhaps unfairly) in the memoirs of Denzil Holles to have been seen at the battle of Alresford hollowing and shouting in a ditch, 'We are undone, we are undone'.

George Wither is a mystery to whom some patient student should one day devote more attention. He was enormously prolific; 'he would make verses as fast as he could write them', says Aubrey.[81] He was also a troublesome man with a grievance, constantly complaining that he had been slighted, neglected and left unpaid. And he was a braggart—St George of Braggadocia as John Taylor called him. Nothing that is known of him sounds very attractive. Yet every so often in the barren acres of his verse there is a stretch enlivened by real wit and observation, or fired with a sudden intensity of feeling. In an attack on half-hearted members of Parliament, written early in the war, he described an election in a way which is not only of social and political interest, but is edged and witty:

> When first this Parliament convened together
> Who called for such as you? How came you hither?
> Confess the truth, are you not some of those,
> Who made the burghers drunk when you were chose?
> Or bribéd them with hopes that when you die
> You would bequeath their town a legacy?
> Or be at least so neighbourly unto them
> As none of those discourtesies to do them,

Which must undoubtedly have been expected
If they your proffered service had neglected
Though now you look upon us as if we
Your vassals and your slaves e'er long should be,
Are not you some of those who came and went
And spake and wrote and sued for our consent?
Are you not they who trotted up and down
To every inn and alehouse in the town
To gain a voice? Did not you for your ends
Crouch to your equals, importune your friends,
Court your inferiors, scrape acquaintance with
Mere strangers, feast the cobbler and the smith,
Nay more, upon the drunken tapster fawn,
And leave your word and promises in pawn
With chamberlains and ostlers, that they might
Be factors for you, being out of sight,
To move their customers who had a voice
To make you objects of their servile choice?[82]

With the end of the first Civil War and the defeat
of the Cavaliers, popular poetry reflected with a kind
of cheerful despair the chaos that had been made of
government, first by the war, then by the increase of
the preaching sects and the quarrel between Presbyterians and Independents. The preaching sects, the
'Impuritans' as John Taylor calls them, with their
'Amsterdamnable opinions' were a favourite target
for criticism. A popular ballad, written by Thomas
Jordan, makes game both of the sects and of the
threatened new democracy:

Come clownes and boyes, come hoberdehoys,
Come Females of each degree,
Stretch your throats, bring in your Votes,
And make good the Anarchy.

> Sure I have the truth, says Numph,
> Nay I ha' the truth sayes Clemme,
> Nay I ha' the truth sayes reverent Ruth,
> Nay I ha' the truth sayes Nem.
> We're fourscore Religions strong
> Then take your choice, the major voice
> Shall carry it right or wrong; . . .
> Then let's ha' King Charles, sayes George
> Nay we'll have his son, sayes Hugh
> Nay then let's ha' none says jabbering Jone,
> Nay lets be all Kings, sayes Prue.[83]

There are more solemn descriptions of the troubled situation of 1647, though none more lively. The only power was that of the sword, and the sword was held by those who, to the conservative civilian, especially if he was a property owner, seemed to be people of extremely dangerous views. The following anonymous lines are addressed to lawyers and others who were trying to get the better of this menacing and indestructible army:

> Lay by your pleading, law lies a bleeding
> Burn all your studies down, and throw away your reading;
> Small power the word has, and can afford us
> Not half so many privileges as the sword has;
> It ventures, it entres, it circles, it centres,
> And makes a prentice free in spite of his indentures,
> This takes off tall things and sets up small things
> This masters money, though money masters all things;
> 'Tis not in season to talk of reason
> Or call it legal when the sword will have it treason?
> It conquers the Crown too, the furs and the gown too,
> This sets up a Presbyter and this pulls him down too,
> This subtle deceiver turns bonnet to beaver,
> Down drops a Bishop, and up starts a weaver.[84]

The more popular Royalist versifiers treated the matter in a lighter vein, but with increasing bitterness. The irrepressibly fertile Alexander Brome, who was now losing his confident gaiety and becoming sour and cynical, shed an unusual light on the New Model Army, the Army of Saints, when he attributed to the Independent soldier the following ambition:

> The *Church* and the *State* we'l turn into Liquor,
> And spend a whole town in a day....[85]

It is certainly an exaggerated picture of the drinking and plundering propensities of the Independents; on the other hand it was commonly and truly said of them by the Presbyterians that they made their religious tenets an excuse for behaving in a more 'frolic fashion' than did the strictly organised and controlled Presbyterians. We have it on the evidence of the slightly shocked Mrs Hutchinson, that Colonel Thomas Harrison, fanatic though he was, wore scarlet and curled his lustrous black hair like any Cavalier.

To these troubled years belong the best works of a man who, given time and better advantages, might have been a major satirist, the London journalist, Marchamont Nedham. For such a prolific writer he has had relatively little notice and nearly all of it disparaging. The kindest thing yet written about him is Sir Charles Firth's article in the *Dictionary of National Biography*. Nedham is a familiar figure on the outskirts of literature at all times; he was a sharp and fluent writer, whose mind ran over with amusing ideas, and who was ready to earn money with his pen regardless of principles. If he had ever had them he had lost them in the struggle to live. He was the kind of feckless hireling who then frequented the eating houses and wine shops of Westminster and the Strand; and is sometimes found to-day propping up a bar in Fleet Street. Oddly enough he had a secondary profession, that of a doctor, and was from time to time driven to exercise it, but he always came back to journalism. He was equally ready in prose and verse. During the war he had worked very well for Parliament as editor of the semi-official *Mercurius Britanicus*, the witty news-sheet which week by week replied to the equally witty *Mercurius Aulicus*, the king's official paper published in Oxford.

The Royalists bitterly resented him, perhaps because he was almost the only Parliamentary journalist who could turn the laugh against them. A mock epitaph on him runs:

> Here lies Britanicus, Hell's barking cur,
> That son of Beliall who kept damned stir;
> And every Munday spent his stocke of spleen
> In venomous railing on the King and Queen.[86]

Suspended and briefly imprisoned by Parliament because he overstepped the mark, 'Hell's barking cur' suddenly turned up in 1647 as principal pro-pagandist for the king, a part he played faithfully throughout the despairing course of the Second Civil War. At this time he issued in parts his rhyming history of the great Rebellion, evading, as many other royalists did, the claws of the censors and their searchers. Like all Nedham's work the rhyming history is very irregular, but it has at its best an angry tingling venom and a sinister, threatening humour which suggests that Nedham was or could have been something much better than a journeyman poet.

He manages to infuse a menacing irony even into such light lines as these, on Puritan prohibition of Christmas festivities:

> All *Plums* the *Prophets Sons* defie,
> And *Spice-broths* are too hot;
> Treason's in a *December-Pye*,
> And Death within the Pot.

> *Christmas*, farewel; thy day (I fear)
> And merry-days are done:
> So they may keep *Feasts* all the year,
> Our *Saviour* shall have none.[87]

This dark underlying anger in Nedham's treatment gives it, on occasion, the power not only to raise a smile, but to chill the marrow: the following verses are his account of the divisions between Parliament, Scots and Army and the mounting threat of force:

> These both agreed to have *no King*;
> The *Scotchman* he goes further,
> *No Bishop*: 'tis a godly thing
> States to reform by Murther.

Then th' *Independent* meek and sly,
Most lowly lies at lurch,
And so to put poor *Jocky* by,
Resolves to have *no Church*.

Our Statesmen (though no Lunaticks,
No *Wizards*, nor *Buffoons*)
Have shewn a hundred Changeling-Tricks,
In less than three New Moons....

O *House* of *Commons*, *House* of *Lords*,
Amend before *September*:
For 'tis *decreed*, your *Souldiers* swords
Shall then you *All-dismember*.[88]

The Second Civil War was marked by the invasion of the Scots, this time in defence of the king, under the incompetent generalship of the Marquis of Hamilton. Hamilton, viewed over the perspective of three hundred years, seems to have been just a very stupid man. But in his own time he had a talent, his only one, for seeming not so much stupid as wicked. He certainly had a facility for changing sides sometimes at the right, more often at the wrong, moment and it was widely held that his ambitious plotting had been responsible for many of the calamities which overtook the king. Of Charles's deep personal attachment to him there is no doubt. So much has to be said in explanation of Nedham's finest and most sinister poem, which he printed at the close of a violent prose pamphlet attacking Hamilton for his alleged betrayals of the king. In spite of the remoteness of the subject, this poem grips at once, partly by its verbal skill, partly because it is so charged with feeling. No one to-day would regard Hamilton as the principal architect of the entire Civil War—but the poem with its ruthless exposure of political ambition still rings true:

> He that three Kingdoms made one flame,
> Blasted their beauty, burn't the frame,
> Himself now here in ashes lies
> A part of this great Sacrifice:...
>
> 'Twas he that first alarm'd the Kirke
> To that prepost'rous bloody worke,
> Upon the *Kings* to place *Christs Throne*,
> A step, and foot-stoole to his owne;
> Taught Zeale a hundred tumbling tricks,
> And Scriptures twin'd with politicks;
> The Pulpit made a Juglers-Box,
> Set Law and Gospell in the Stocks....
> 'Twas he patch't up the new Divine
> Part *Calvin*, and part *Catiline*,
> Could too trans-forme (without a Spell)
> *Satan* into a *Gabriel*;
> Just like those pictures, which we paint
> On this side *Fiend*, on that side *Saint*.
> Both this, and that, and ev'rything
> He was; for, and against the King;
> Rather than he his ends would misse
> Betray'd his *Master* with a *kisse*,
> And buri'd in one common Fate
> The glory of our *Church* and *State*.[89]

Nedham's career did not end with the Royalist defeat in the Second Civil War. He was a principal pamphleteer in Cromwell's interest in the 1650's, and was scribbling usefully for King Charles II after 1660.

So far the Cavaliers had had the best of the verbal battle; they were wittier in condemnation than their opponents, louder in mockery, and in defeat tenaciously defiant. They could still rejoice in the divisions of their enemies. They still made legitimate if rather bitter fun of the vices which usually flourish at a time of social disorder, when the unscrupulous make profits out of their less fortunate and more honest neighbours. It is not unusual with political verse to find it flowing with greater vigour from the opposition.

The trial and execution of the king inspired one or two bold writers and printers to issue elegies and lamentations, but the censorship was growing more ferocious and more efficient and few have survived. Most of the poems—and there were many—written on this theme by Royalist poets were circulated in manuscript. One of the best known at the time was an eight-line stanza on the King's death:

> Great, good and just, could I but rate,
> My grief and thy too rigid fate,
> I'd weep the world in such a strain,
> As it should deluge once again:
> But since thy loud tongued blood demands supplies
> More from Briareus hands than Argus eyes
> I'll tune thy elegies to trumpet sounds
> And write thy epitaph with blood and wounds.[90]

It is not precisely a popular piece but it strongly appealed to the irreconcilables among the Cavaliers, was widely circulated during the Commonwealth and set to music by Samuel Pepys among others. The lines were early ascribed to Montrose, above whose name they appear in the 1653 edition of Cleveland's poems, with those of other wits. There is thus no valid reason for doubting the story of George Wishart, Montrose's chaplain, who asserts that his master wrote the verse immediately after hearing of the king's death.

Another poem on the king's death is ascribed to Cleveland with reasonable probability, though it is more contemplative than his usual manner. It appeared in 1649, unsigned, and very eloquently summed up the idea of the king, as saint and martyr, which was to remain the official and unshaken Royalist view. He had lost his earthly crown to gain an imperishable crown in heaven. We are to imagine him lonely on the scaffold, a defenceless victim, among armed and resolute men:

> Death had no sting for him and its sharp arm,
> Only of all the troop, meant him no harm.
> And so he looked upon the axe as one
> Weapon yet left to guard him to his throne.
> In his great name then may his subjects cry,
> 'Death, thou art swallowed up in victory.'...
>
> His crown was fallen unto too low a thing
> For him who was become so great a King....

99   7-2

> And thus his soul, of this her triumph proud,
> Broke like a flash of lightning through the cloud
> Of flesh and blood; and from the highest line
> Of human virtue, passed to be divine.[91]

The same idea of the king's triumph in death was worked out in a touching poem which may be the work of Henry King, bishop of Chichester. The poem which is over five hundred lines long contains a very sufficient summary of the Civil War from the Royalist point of view. It is couched in the form of an address to the king's enemies, and the Royalist author once again adopts the method that more light-hearted Cavaliers had used in their satirical works earlier in the war—that of quoting the statements made by the Parliamentarians and then giving them a different kind of meaning. It had been the claim of the Parliamentarians at the beginning of the war that if the king would accede to their demands they would make him 'a great and glorious King'. Brome had picked this up in *The Clean Contrary Way*. Now, in tragic mood, Henry King used the same device to conclude his poem:

> Yet have You kept your word against Your will,
> Your King is great indeed and glorious still,
> And you have made Him so. We must impute
> That lustre which His sufferings contribute
> To your preposterous wisdoms, who have done
> All your good deeds by contradiction:
> For as to work his peace you raised this strife,
> And often shot at Him to save His life;

As you took from Him to increase His wealth,
And kept Him prisoner to secure His health;
So in revenge of your dissembled spite,
In this last wrong you did Him greatest right,
And (cross to all You meant) by plucking down,
Lifted Him up to His Eternal Crown.[92]

By far the most famous lines on the king's death occur in Marvell's *Horatian Ode on Cromwell's return from Ireland*, written presumably in the summer of 1650, but not published until thirty years later. Marvell's political attitude at this time is an enigma, which this poem with its restrained and almost ironic attitude to Cromwell does not solve. He had not fought in the war; he had been abroad. He was within a year or two to become a member of the household of Fairfax, the Parliamentarian general. Later he was to be one of Cromwell's sincerest admirers. Yet we owe to him the most quoted lines in our language on the death of Charles:

> *He* nothing common did or mean
> Upon that memorable Scene:
> But with his keener Eye
> The Axes edge did try:
> Nor call'd the *Gods* with vulgar spight
> To vindicate his helpless Right,
> But bow'd his comely Head,
> Down as upon a Bed.[93]

It is strange how small details noticed by eye-witnesses on the scaffold are caught up into this poem—for it is recorded by one that he had never seen the king's eyes brighter than in his last moments, and by another that he more than once inquired about the sharpness of the axe.

Marvell at that time stood aloof; later he was to voice strong and well-defined Puritan opinions. This poem is puzzling, indeed it is eccentric, in its objectivity at a time when passions were so deeply engaged. Many, if not most, thinking men then in England felt the earth shake under them when a king was executed on a public scaffold. We to-day, more accustomed to revolutionary shocks, can be easily misled by the boldness and modernity of certain seventeenth-century democratic ideas. But such ideas were held by a very small, if a very vocal minority. In general the people, from highest to lowest, were conventional and bound by strong and ancient traditions as to what was morally and what was socially right. The murder of a king was infinitely shocking to the majority of them, and they feared the judgment of God on such appalling impiety. In this context of thought Marvell's lines, with their lofty and dignified and strangely unconcerned vision, show a mind of great strength and originality.

Abraham Cowley, shaken to the core of his being by the king's murder, sloughed off almost completely the elaborations of his earlier manner, and apostrophised the Almighty in a prayer for his sinful and perhaps doomed country:

> Yet mighty God, yet yet, we humbly crave,
> This floating Isle from shipwrack save;
> And though to wash that Bloud which does it stain,
> It well deserves to sink into the Main;
> Yet for the Royal Martyr's prayer
> (The Royal Martyr prays we know)
> This guilty, perishing Vessel spare;
> Hear but his Soul above, and not his bloud below....

To Cowley—as to other Royalists—the most horrible thing of all was that the act had been perpetrated by a small group of his own deluded countrymen who, in spite of their guilt, were suffered to control and govern the rest. This was worse to bear than any previous conquest or any other curse of heaven—

> Come rather Pestilence and reap us down;
> Come Gods sword, rather than our own.
> Let rather *Roman* come again,
> Or *Saxon*, *Norman*, or the *Dane*,
> In all the bonds we ever bore,
> We griev'd, we sigh'd, we wept; we never blusht before.[94]

This no longer sounds like the elegant pastoral Cowley who summoned ten thousand Cupids to scatter oriental perfumes on the field of Edgehill. His cry of anguish can fittingly close the commentary of the poets on the epoch of the Civil Wars. A devoted Royalist to the end, he could see no virtues in the Commonwealth government. Yet it was a government for which better poets, if not better men, than Cowley would find no cause to blush.

IV

THE VANQUISHED AND
THE VICTORS

The immediate effect on the Royalists of the king's death—or, to use their own word for it, the king's murder—was to inspire an heroic passion for the service of his son. This passion, which could be freely expressed by the Cavaliers in exile, was also, in a variety of transparent disguises, set forth in unlicensed broadsheets circulated in England without authors' or printers' names. The ballad of *The Weeping Widow*, though the lady remains anonymous, clearly refers to Queen Henrietta Maria; more outspoken is *The Royal Health to the Rising Sun* with its refrain: 'The sun that sets, may after rise again'; or *The Twelve Brave Bells of Bow* which contains such lines as:

> *Jove* with his traine
> Supporteth Charles's Waine
> Although the dog-star grin and sore doe bite;

and has one explicit reference to 'rare Charles the second of that name'.[95]

Slightly later comes the oddly titled *Ladies Lamentation for the loss of her Landlord*; this is the lament of a love-lorn lass for someone whom she calls her 'blackbird most royal' (the swarthy complexion of Charles II is here intended, as also in his more frequent nickname the Black Boy). The refrain, 'I'll find out my true love wherever he be', is simply a pledge of eternal loyalty to the exiled young king.[96]

The fervour of the Royalists was no substitute for unity. Their councils were divided and their actions abroad and at home fatally weakened by those disagreements and recriminations which are apt to break out among the exiled and defeated. In any case all the anonymous ballad-mongers in England would hardly have prevailed against an efficient armed force. Furthermore there had always been among the Cavaliers a strain of light-heartedness, a willingness to dismiss dull care and call for a drink. This is all very well for a triumphant party; it may even have been helpful while the fortunes of war seemed to incline in their favour, but it very easily turned sour when things went amiss. The disintegration of the Cavaliers in defeat can be followed with horrid clarity through some of their favourite songs.

On the eve of the war Richard Lovelace had been imprisoned for presenting a petition to Parliament. This was the occasion on which he composed his most famous poem: *To Althea from Prison*. It was not published until 1649, but it had been already circulating in manuscript for several years, and had established a type of poem that was increasingly popular with the Cavaliers as the darkness closed in on their cause and more and more of them saw the inside of prisons. None of the imitations comes at all near to the beauty of the original, and the theme, as the years went by, was treated with increasing crudity.

Lovelace built his poem on a typically Caroline conceit, the antithesis of the liberty that he enjoyed in his mistress' favour and the imprisonment of his body; he decorated it with such pretty trivialities as that of lying 'tangled in her hair and fettered to her eye'. But his verses move on, by way of such common prison pastimes as drinking and singing with his friends, to a statement about the triumph of mind over matter simple and profound, limpid and musical, which has rightly become one of the most quoted verses in the whole of English literature:

> Stone walls do not a prison make
> Nor iron bars a cage;
> Minds innocent and quiet take
> This for an hermitage;
> If I have freedom in my love
> And in my soul am free;
> Angels alone, that soar above,
> Enjoy such liberty.

This is a poem about a particular man imprisoned for a particular reason; it arises directly from the political circumstances of the time in which it was written, but it transcends the temporary and lifts Lovelace to the immortals.

In the imitations written on the same theme this noble element is gradually weakened; there is a good deal about loyalty, more about mistresses, still more about drink. Thus:

> These Mannacles upon my Arme,
> I as my Mistris's favours weare;
> And for to keep my Ankles warm,
> I have some Iron Shackles there.
> > These walls are but my garrison; this Cell
> > Which men call Goal, doth prove my Cittadel.

Or thus:

> Come pass about the *bowl* to me,
> A health to our distressed King;
> Though we're in hold, let cups go free,
> Birds in a *cage* may freely sing.[97]

Those lines still have a certain gallant spirit to them, but very soon the theme of a man's spiritual liberty while his body is confined, drops away into a mere statement that drink is the cure to all evils. As in this by Alexander Brome:

Into prison we get,
For the crime called *debt*,...
Where our ditties still be: *give's more drink*, gives' more drink, boyes,
Our *Gaolers* and we, will live by our chink boys,
While our *Creditors* live by the air....[98]

It may be said with some truth that to be a gallant soldier in prison and to be in prison for debt are clean different things, though both happened to Royalists for much the same cause. But it is worth recalling that, though Victorian anthologists by calling Lovelace 'Colonel' have conspired to make us think of him as a soldier, he was in prison for nothing more dramatic than a breach of privilege of Parliament, and he scarcely drew sword in the Civil War at all.

But it is unhappily true that the financial oppression of the defeated Cavaliers was one reason that some of them found themselves in debtors' prisons, and men are notoriously more easily demoralised by squalid hole-and-corner embarrassments than by much worse sufferings endured openly and directly for a cause. Decay and disintegration of the Cavalier spirit was probably inevitable as the result of economic pressure. It found a poet of a kind in Alexander Brome, whose work deserves study if only for the lamentable comment which it supplies under its apparent lightness on the rotting away of a cause. He began as a brisk rhymester of Cavalier victories and a cheerful satirist of the Roundheads. During the Commonwealth he was the most popular voice of the oppressed Cavaliers still in England and his sour little songs, circulated in manuscript or by word of mouth, were eloquent of a bitterness which, in the end, lacks all nobility and degenerates to an ill-tempered sneer:

> That side is always right that's strong
> And that that's beaten must be wrong;
> And he that thinks it is not so
> Unless he's sure to beat them too
> Is but a fool to oppose 'em,

and again:

> Those *politick would-bees* do but shew themselves asses,
> That other mens calling invade,
> We only converse with pots and with glasses;
> Let the Rulers alone with their trade.

Or this harsh credo:

> What is't to us who's is the ruling power?
> *While they protect, we're bound to obey,*
> But longer, not an hour
>
> Each wise man first best loves himself,
> Lives close, thinks and obeys;
> Makes not his soul a slave to's pelf;
> Nor idly squanders it away,
> To cram their mawes that taxes lay,
> On what he does or sayes;
> For those grand cords that man to man do twist,
> Now are not honesty and love
> But self and interest.[99]

In the early days of the troubles, the Cavalier soldier, James Smith, had written

> And now, like wandring Knights we wend
> Without a penny, or a friend:
> Our score growes great, from whence we goe,
> And every alehouse turn'd a foe....[100]

It is difficult to keep up any of the more pleasing attributes of wandering knights when money to pay for the next drink becomes the principal concern.

Early in the Commonwealth, Brome wrote some commendatory verses to Lovelace in which he spoke of:

> ...the thick darkness of these verseless times
> These *antigenius* dayes, this boystrous age,
> Where there dwells nought of Poetry but rage.... [101]

But rage might have brought forth something more memorable, and is perhaps a less degrading sentiment, than the empty disillusionment that gradually came to replace it.

Disillusionment, hopelessness at least, was not among the vices of the much-divided victors of the war who were faced after the king's execution with the business of refashioning the government and re-uniting the three kingdoms—since Scotland and Ireland for different reasons each rejected the republican dispensation. Their vices were of another kind. The Royalist taunt, uttered with increasing vehemence ever since the war had begun, that they enriched themselves, was true of some of them. A winning side always attracts to it the ambitious and the time-serving and there were evidently pickings to be had from the mulcting of the defeated. The greatest poet among them, in one of the rare sonnets of these years, seems to admit the Royalist charge, and to see in the purification of such abuses the first task which lay ahead of the victors when the war was won. That I take to be the meaning of the lines

addressed by John Milton to Fairfax at the close of
the Second Civil War:

> *Fairfax*, whose name in arms through Europe rings
> Filling each mouth with envy, or with praise,
> And all her jealous monarchs with amaze,
> And rumors loud, that daunt remotest kings,
> Thy firm unshak'n vertue ever brings
> Victory home, though new rebellions raise
> Their Hydra heads, and the fals North displaies
> Her brok'n league, to impe their serpent wings,
> O yet a nobler task awaites thy hand;
> For what can Warr but endless warr still breed,
> Till Truth, and Right from Violence be freed,
> And Public Faith cleard from the shamefull brand
> Of Public Fraud. In vain doth Valour bleed
> While Avarice, and Rapine share the land.[102]

'Public Faith cleard from the shamefull brand Of
Public Fraud' recalls the Royalist Cowley's ironical
reflections some years before on the exploitation by
Parliament of this term the 'public faith' and the
small probability that any who lent money on that
guarantee would ever get it back again. Milton's
sonnet—not published until after his death—shows
how keenly the high-minded were aware of the corruption and evils within their cause. But in the
years immediately succeeding the king's death, the
necessity of consolidating government in England,
ending the revolt in Ireland, and bringing the Scots
under control, prevented attention to the nobler
task. The Cavaliers and indifferents could still mock
at the victors, and deride a government more con-

fused, and, financially speaking, more oppressive, than the king's had been. In a farewell to London, Brome makes the Cavaliers say:

> Now we must desert thee,
> With the lines that begirt thee,
> And the red-coated Saints domineer
> Who with Liberty fool thee,
> While a Monster doth rule thee,
> And thou feels't what before thou didst fear....[103]

The 'monster' is the Rump 'where thirty fools and twenty knaves make up a Parliament', as Marchamont Nedham not quite accurately puts it. The Royalists also at this time unpacked their hearts by railing at the low birth of their new ruler:

> Like frogs of Nilus from an inundation
> Raised out of plunder and of sequestration....

Cromwell appears constantly as the brewer, from his descent from Williams the Putney brewer, and on one occasion as 'bold Bellona's Brewer'. But even the Royalists greeted his expulsion of the Rump with pleasure:

> The Parliament sate as snug as a Cat,
> And were playing for mine and yours:
> Sweep-stakes was their Game, till *Oliver* came,
> And turn'd it to Knave out of doors....[104]

But alongside the confusion of government there was a tremendous confidence in the God-directed mission of the English Puritans. The self-assured fervour of their popular verses contrasts favourably with the thin sneering of the defeated Cavaliers. The suppression of the Irish rebellion and the defeat of the Scots at Dunbar, and finally at Worcester, had a spiritual as well as a purely material effect. If it had really been a blasphemy against God's order on earth to kill the king, as many people in all classes thought at the time, then God showed his disapprobation in a very strange way. None of the unspeakable calamities that were feared or predicted came to pass. The 'red-coated Saints' went on to victories so overwhelming and so remarkable that those who were quick, as our forefathers were, to see signs and omens in such things could not but be impressed by what looked like the blessing, if not the intervention, of the Almighty.

The first shattering blow to Royalist hopes had been in Ireland, when—before the landing of Cromwell—General Michael Jones, cut off in Dublin, without any present hope of relief, won at Rathmines a sudden, unexpected and overwhelming victory against far superior forces, a blow from which the Irish and Anglo-Irish Royalists never recovered. George Wither celebrated this incident in a poem which conveys with great vividness the Puritan confidence in God's intervention and indeed the identification of the English with the Chosen People. Some of Wither's lines also show, in their censorious attitude to Cavalier gaiety, that the characteristics celebrated in Alexander Brome's songs could appear to a hostile witness as evidence of deep inward guilt.

Wither begins with a bold description of how Michael Jones and his men won the day—

> *Mich'el* and his *Angells*, there
> Threw their *Dragon-Cavaliere*,
> With his *Angells*, from our *Sphere*...

and then proceeds to this:

> For, though (blinded by their sin)
> *Outwardly*, they jeer and grin;
> Hellish horrors lurk within,
>   Filling their faint hearts with fears.
> Their *chief refuge*, is a *lie*;
> And, which way soe'er they fly,
> *Guilt* pursues them with a cry,
>   Which the God of Justice hears.
> Their accusing *conscience*, feels
> *Vengeance* following them at heels,
> And, her dreadfull Charet wheels
>   Threatning, what to them is due....

Next Wither describes his own side:

> Oh! what pen or tongue is there
> Fully able to declare,
> What, to us, GOD's *Mercies* were
>   Since our *Champion* he hath been?
> Nay, who can half that recite,
> Which for us, in open sight,
> He hath done since *Naseby-Fight*,
>   Where, he, first, was plainly seen?
>
> He hath magnifi'd his *worth*
> In most glorious marchings forth,

From the *South*, unto the *North*,
    And, through all our *British Coasts*;
England, *Scotland*, *Ireland*, *Wales*,
Towns, and *Fields*, and *Hills*, and *Dales*,
Sea, and *Land* him, justly calls
The Victorious Lord of Hoasts.

We have seen God marching, so,
With our *Friends*, against our *Foe*,
As he did, long time ago,
    When His Isr'el was opprest;
And, securing us from feare;
When our hopes at lowest were;
When despis'd, we did appeare,
    And our peril most increast.

We have seen the pride of *Kings*,
With those much desired things,
Whence their vain ambition springs,
    Scorn'd, despis'd, and set at naught.
We, their *silk*, their *pearls*, their *gold*,
And their *precious* Jems, behold,
Scattred, pawnéd, bought and sold;
    And to shame, their glory brought.

We have seen God, in our daies,
Walking on, in all those waies,
Which (to his eternall praise)
    Were in *former Ages* trod:
In our joyes, and when we *weep*,
In our *wakings*, in our *sleep*,
On the Heights, and in the Deep
    We have seen thy steps O GOD.[105]

This conviction that God had called his Englishmen supplied the motive force for the extraordinary

resurgence of England under Cromwell. The nation once again began to exert a European influence after a long period of eclipse. The change of atmosphere, the astonishment of European powers who for twenty years had regarded England as negligible, and finally the renewed concentration on sea-power which characterised the rule of Cromwell is admirably conveyed in Marvell's poem in praise of him on the first anniversary of his Protectorate. He imagines rival European powers discussing England:

> Is this, saith one, the Nation that we read
> Spent with both Wars, under a Captain dead?
> Yet rig a Navy while we dress us late;
> And ere we Dine, rase and rebuild their State.
> What Oaken Forrests, and what golden Mines!
> What Mints of Men, what Union of Designes!...
> Theirs are not Ships, but rather Arks of War,
> And beaked Promontories sail'd from far;
> Of floting Islands a new Hatched Nest;
> A Fleet of Worlds, of other Worlds in quest;...
> Needs must we all their Tributaries be,
> Whose Navies hold the Sluces of the Sea.[106]

In the same poem Marvell compares the emergence of Cromwell, to stabilise and rule a nation deluged by war, to the natural power which fell to Noah as the survivor of the flood. The poem is typical Marvell in its amalgamation of the dominant ideas of the time: the works of God and nature reflected in government. It begins with a justification of Cromwell against the charge of tyranny:

> 'Tis not a Freedome, that where All command;
> Nor Tyranny, where One does them withstand:
> But who of both, the Bounders knows to lay—
> Him as their Father must the State obey.
>   Thou, and thine House, like *Noah*'s Eight did rest,
> Left by the Wars Flood on the Mountains crest:
> And the large Vale lay subject to thy Will,
> Which thou but as an Husbandman wouldst Till:
> And only didst for others plant the Vine
> Of Liberty, not drunken with its Wine.[107]

From then on the tide of poetic praise which rises towards Cromwell equals that which had flowed twenty years before to King Charles, with this essential difference that there was more justification in Cromwell's case.

> Illustrious acts high raptures do infuse,
> And every conqueror creates a muse,[108]

wrote Edmund Waller. Conveniently forgetting that his muse had been inspired in his youth to hail Charles I on very scanty evidence as conqueror of the abounding main, he now in middle age celebrated in a *Panegyric to my Lord Protector* the greatness of Cromwell and England's command of the sea—

> The sea's our own; and now all nations greet,
> With bending sails, each vessel of our fleet;
> Your power extends as far as winds can blow,
> Or swelling sails upon the globe may go.
>
> Heaven (that hath placed this island to give law,
> To balance Europe, and her states to awe)
> In this conjunction does on Britain smile;
> The greatest leader, and the greatest isle!

> Hither the oppresséd shall henceforth resort,
> Justice to crave, and succour, at your court;
> And then your Highness, not for ours alone,
> But for the world's protector shall be known.
>
> As the vexed world, to find repose, at last
> Itself into Augustus' arms did cast;
> So England now does, with like toil oppressed,
> Her weary head upon your bosom rest....[109]

It is not very easy to admire poor Waller as a man, though he may be legitimately admired as a poet. Yet he probably wrote at this time with a very fair degree of sincerity, for the Cromwellian government brought a sufficient measure of prosperity at home, and that respect from European nations of which the English had been starved since Elizabethan days. The London populace, the weathercock of public opinion, reacted very quickly to the new situation, much enjoying this kind of doggerel:

> We have as brave a Navy
> As ever bore up saile
> We have as brave Commanders,
> As ever did prevaile:
> We have a brave Land Army,
> Of Souldiers as 'tis found,
> No bolder sparks did ever breathe
> Nor tread on English ground....[110]

This was the superficial mood of the middle 1650's, and this resurgent aggressive patriotism was by no means all aggressive. The sense of mission so

clear in Wither's poem on the victory at Rathmines
was an important element. The old conception of
England as the defender of oppressed Protestantism
emerged vigorously when the Duke of Savoy
massacred his unfortunate Vaudois subjects. The
news-sheets were full of the atrocity; it was the
subject of at least one ballad. It inspired Milton to
the most powerful of his political sonnets.

> Avenge O Lord thy slaughter'd Saints, whose bones
> Lie scatter'd on the Alpine mountains cold,
> Ev'n them who kept thy truth so pure of old
> When all our Fathers worship't Stocks and Stones,
> Forget not: in thy book record their groanes
> Who were thy Sheep and in their antient fold
> Slayn by the bloody *Piemontese* that roll'd
> Mother with Infant down the Rocks. Their moans
> The Vales redoubl'd to the Hills, and they
> To Heav'n. Their martyr'd blood and ashes sow
> O'er all th' *Italian* fields where still doth sway
> The triple Tyrant: that from these may grow
> A hunder'd-fold, who having learnt thy way
> Early may fly the *Babylonian* wo.[III]

This fervid sense of the national mission was not,
however, of any long duration, or at least not with
the majority. Nothing could, in the long run, give
any appearance of permanency to the evidently
interim regime of Cromwell, nothing could reconcile
the majority of the nation to the sheer illegality and
irregularity of their government. In spite of the deep
draughts of the heady wine of national pride, the
country remained uneasy, divided and seamed with

plots. A growing anxiety about the future darkened the closing years of Cromwell's rule.

His death was none the less greeted by Marvell, by Waller and by others with elegiac regret. Marvell's *Poem on the Death of the Protector* is not one of his greatest works, but it contains some touching and some finely descriptive passages, and of its sincerity we are not left for a moment in doubt. Marvell constantly emphasises those things about Cromwell which, from personal knowledge of him during the years of the Commonwealth, he had come to admire—his temperate and merciful nature, his desire for peace—

> He whom nature all for peace had made
> But angry heaven unto war had swayed....

His family affections and his relations with his daughter Elizabeth are tenderly, almost humorously, described—

> While she with smiles serene, in words discreet,
> His hidden soul at every turn could meet.

There is no suggestion in this poem, as there is in the *Horatian Ode*, written before he was a convinced Cromwellian, that Cromwell, though essentially an instrument of fate, had also a vein of sly ambition in him. The figure Marvell drew in the *Horatian Ode* was the human tool of powers greater than he; but in the poem on Cromwell's death, Cromwell himself has become a force of nature, linked to the elements, while still retaining certain noble and massive human characteristics. This very long poem was conceived, like all that Marvell wrote, as an organic whole so that fragmentary quotation hardly does it justice: but here is the storm, and the fatal, glorious date of 3 September:

The great Protector is sinking fast—
He without noise still travelled to his end
As silent suns to meet the night descend.
The stars that for him fought had only power
Left to determine now his fatal hour
Which since they might not hinder, yet they cast
To choose it worthy of his glories past.
No part of time but bare his mark away
Of honour—all the year was Cromwell's day.
But this of all the most auspicious found
Twice had in open field him victor crown'd
When up the arméd mountains of Dunbar
He marched, and through deep Severn, ending war:
What day should him eternise but the same
That had before immortalised his name.

O Cromwell, Heaven's favourite, to none
Have such high honours from above been shown.
For whom the elements we mourners see
And Heaven itself would the great herald be....

Later comes the splendid passage on the fighting fervour of the Ironsides:

He first put arms into religion's hand
And timorous conscience unto courage mann'd,
The soldier taught that inward mail to wear
And fearing God how they should nothing fear,
Those strokes he said will pierce through all below
Where those that strike from Heaven fetch their blow;

> Astonish'd armies did their flight prepare
> And cities strong were storméd by his prayer;
> Of that forever Preston's field shall tell
> The story, and impregnable Clonmel.

Impregnable Clonmel and all too pregnable Drogheda and Wexford have from that day to this in the bitter memory of the Irish told the story, though not in the terms that Andrew Marvell had in mind.

Finally the slow, tragic lines which, like so much in this poem, record the impact of personal experience:

> I saw him dead, a leaden slumber lyes,
> And mortal sleep over those wakefull eyes:
> Those gentle rays under the lids were fled,
> Which through his looks that piercing sweetnesse shed;
> That port which so majestique was and strong,
> Loose and depriv'd of vigour, stretch'd along:
> All wither'd, all discolour'd, pale and wan,
> How much another thing, no more that man![112]

Compared with the genuine grief of Marvell, the lamentations of Waller who hurried an elegy into print are altogether too brisk and professional. Of the fearful storm he writes glibly:

> We must resign! Heaven his great soul does claim
> In storms, as loud as his immortal fame;
> His dying groans, his last breath, shakes our isle,
> And trees uncut fall for his funeral pile....

Like Marvell, he devotes some lines to the revived glories of England achieved by Cromwell's foreign policy:

The ocean, which so long our hopes confined,
Could give no limits to his vaster mind;
Our bounds' enlargement was his latest toil,
Nor hath he left us prisoners to our isle;
Under the tropic is our language spoke,
And part of Flanders hath received our yoke.
From civil broils he did us disengage,
Found nobler objects for our martial rage;
And with wise conduct to his country showed
Their ancient way of conquering abroad.[113]

For some reason, George Wither who was getting old and increasingly crotchety took exception not only to Waller's elegy but to pretty well everything written about Cromwell's death, whether because he was now out of humour with the man whom he had once hailed as the 'bright lode star of the North', or because he was indignant at the repressive measures of the last months of Cromwell's rule. He took up Waller very sharply:

What *Comfort* yields it, to impose a *Yoke*
On others, if our *fetters* be not broke?
What *Pleasure* brings it, if our *Confines* be
Inlarged, if in them, we are not free?[114]

A new young poet, contributing heroic stanzas on Cromwell's death, defied all the doubts and uncertainties of the times with this conclusion, after thirty stanzas lucidly and efficiently devoted to the Protector's triumphs abroad:

No Civil Broils have since his Death arose,
But Faction now, by Habit, does obey;
And Wars have that Respect for his Repose,
As winds for *Halcyons*, when they breed at Sea.

His Ashes in a Peaceful Urn shall rest,
His Name a great Example stands to show,
How strangely high Endeavours may be bless'd,
Where Piety and Valour jointly go.[115]

Those lines were written by John Dryden, twenty-nine years old and following what still seemed to be the fashion. He was not at his happiest here either as poet or prophet, since the Commonwealth government took only a few months to disintegrate, and Cromwell's ashes would not long rest in peace.

From the rapid collapse of Cromwell's son, Richard, the Cavaliers gathered new hope, and Alexander Brome had almost a flash of his old, bold briskness in political comment. For him, of course, the turns and changes in the state, the tragic, frantic manœuvres of the supporters of the Good Old Cause were merely so many selfish moves of men anxious to keep their wealth and power. In a heartless little squib at their expense he made mock of the rather too frequently used seventeenth-century formula of swearing 'to live and die' with some particular leader or party. His *dramatis personae* include Sir Arthur Haslerig the veteran protagonist of republicanism, John Lambert the most ambitious of Cromwell's generals, and finally the restored Rump of the Long Parliament. The lines give a graphic picture of the quick political turnover of the months after Cromwell's death:

But I'm concerned (methinks) to find
Our *Grandees* turn with every wind,
Yet keep like Corks above:
They lived and died but two years since
With *Oliver* their pious Prince,
Whom they did fear and *love*.

As soon as *Richard* did but raign,
They liv'd and dy'd with him again,
And *swore* to serve him ever:
But when Sir *Arthur* came with's men
They liv'd and dy'd with him agen,
Dick had been never.

And when *Prince Lambert* turn'd them out,
They liv'd and dy'd another bout,
And vilifi'd the *Rump*:
And now for them they *live* and *dye*,
But for the *Devil* by and by
If he turn'd up *Trump*.[116]

It was not the Devil who turned up trump but the
exiled king.

The Restoration of King Charles II was welcomed
by more poems and ballads than any other event of
the century, and most of them contained tributes to
General George Monk whose ingenuity, level-
headedness and good sense in solving the political
problem without bloodshed lent itself to a variety of
simple or sophisticated comparisons. The ballad-
mongers made obvious play with his Christian name,
associating him with St George and the Dragon.
One writer, John Collop, puns on his surname,

Our English Monk hath here converted more
Than all your monks perverted heretofore.[117]

John Dryden, straining a great deal too hard, compares the operations of Monk in bringing about the Restoration, to the painter's subtle brush strokes which

> by one slight touch restore
> Smiles to that changed face that wept before;

to the skilled patience of an angler, and to the work of the digestive juices in the body.[118]

Waller, taking the more obvious simile of the Gordian knot, is less original, but neater and happier:

> If then such praise the Macedonian got
> For having rudely cut the Gordian knot,
> What glory's due to him that could divide
> Such ravelled interests; has the knot untied
> And without stroke, so smooth a passage made
> Where craft and malice such impeachment laid?

Waller's poem on the king's return is throughout impressively skilful, not least in the manner in which he covers his own rapid change of politics since he had wept over Cromwell's bier. He excuses himself by attributing the same fickle guilt to the whole nation. He approaches the point circuitously, thus:

> The rising sun complies with our weak sight,
> First gilds the clouds, then shows his globe of light
> At such a distance from our eyes, as though
> He knew what harm his hasty beams would do.
> But your full Majesty at once breaks forth
> In the meridian of your reign. Your worth,
> Your youth, and all the splendours of your state,
> (Wrapped up till now in clouds of adverse fate!)

With such a flood of light invade our eyes,
And our spread hearts with so great joy surprise,
That if your grace incline that we should live,
You must not, sir! too hastily forgive.
Our guilt preserves us from excess of joy,
Which scatters spirits, and would life destroy.
All are obnoxious! and this faulty land,
Like fainting Esther, does before you stand,
Watching your sceptre. The revolted sea
Trembles to think she did your foes obey.[119]

A fault committed even by the sea ought obviously to be forgiven in Waller, whose references to 'fainting Esther' do at least show a certain consciousness that he was in a precarious position.

As a young courtier poet he had over-topped his contemporaries in praise of Charles I; in the Long Parliament he had joined the opposition to the king, then involved himself in a plot on the king's behalf and bought his pardon when he was discovered while five of his companions were hanged on his evidence; lastly under Cromwell he had published lavish praise of the government. No wonder he felt a little anxious in 1660.

The young Dryden who had done nothing worse than grow up and show his earliest poetical paces in politeness to the Cromwellian regime also touched on this delicate point in his poem to the returning king, 'Astraea Redux'.

But since, reform'd by what we did amiss,
We by our suff'rings learn to prize our bliss.

> Like early Lovers, whose unpractis'd hearts
> Were long the May-game of malicious arts,
> When once they find their Jealousies were vain,
> With double heat renew their Fires again.

After this strangely unsuitable image of Cromwell playing a may-game of malicious arts with the English people, Dryden prettily concludes with an appeal to the king:

> So tears of Joy for your returning spilt,
> Work out and expiate our former Guilt.[120]

In the general din, the infant voice of the Earl of Rochester, aged twelve, was uplifted to greet the king, and to remind him that he was son to that Harry Wilmot who had accompanied Charles II on his dangerous flight after the battle of Worcester. Rochester's 'one ambition 'tis for to be known, by daring loyalty your Wilmot's son'. The poem, although conventional, has certain strokes of original observation.

> And Loyal Kent renews her arts agen,
> Fencing her ways with moving Groves of Men

is a graphic description of roads lined with hastening, cheering multitudes.[121]

Rochester would make his way by his own merits or demerits, not by his father's. It was very soon apparent that the turncoats had nothing to fear and the loyalists very little to hope from the returning king. Alexander Brome, speaking for the bedraggled

and decayed Cavaliers, sums up their last and most
bitter disappointment:

> We have laid all at stake
> For his Majesty's sake,
> We have fought, we have paid,
> We've been sold and betrayed,
> And tumbled from nation to nation;
> But now those are thrown down
> That usurp'd the Crown,
> Our hopes were that we
> All rewarded should be,
> But we're paid with a Proclamation.

The king's proclamation of Oblivion and Indemnity
was popularly said to be of Oblivion to his friends
and Indemnity to his enemies. Brome goes on:

> Now the times are turn'd about
> And the Rebels race is run:
> That many headed beast, the Rout,
> Who did turn the Father out
> When they saw they were undon,
> Were for bringing in the Son.
> The phanatical crue
> Which made us all rue,
> Have got so much wealth,
> By their plunder and stealth,
> That they creep into profit and power:
> And so come what will
> They'll be uppermost still;
> And we that are low
> Shall still be kept so
> While those domineer and devour.[122]

Another rhyme, from an anonymous writer, this
time imagines two 'old rusty Cavaliers' talking over

a visit to Whitehall where they have seen not one
familiar face.

> Not one, upon my life, among
> My old acquaintance, all along
> At *Truro*, and before;
> And, I suppose the Place can shew
> As few of those, whom thou didst know
> At *York* and *Marston Moore*.

On this sad evidence they agree that:

> Old services, (by rule of state)
> Like *Almanacks*, grow out of date.[123]

This new ungrateful, light-hearted society read
and delighted in the most famous of all the attacks
on the now defeated Puritans, Samuel Butler's
Hudibras. Pepys bought it for 2*s*. 6*d*. on 26 December
1662, but at first thought nothing of it and passed
it on to a friend for eighteen pence. In a few weeks
it was so much the common talk of the town and so
much cried up by everyone that he had to buy it
again.[124]

Samuel Butler had known and been influenced by
the most sophisticated satirist writing during the
war, John Cleveland, and as a silent resentful
Royalist during the Commonwealth he had been
familiar with the Cavalier lampoons and mockeries.
Hudibras was the final product of Civil War satire,
the strong-water ultimately distilled from the plentiful coarse, angry, comic, impulsive, ingenious,
quick-off-the-mark rhymes that the Cavalier wits

had written against their opponents as the conflict proceeded.

Repeatedly Butler took up, sharpened and perfected ideas and themes which had been roughly sketched out before. For instance he mocked at Parliament's changes of policy or their protestations of loyalty to the king whom they were fighting.

> Did not our *Worthies* of the *House*,
> Before they broke the *Peace*, break *Vows*?
> For having freed us, first, from both
> Th'*Allegiance* and *Supremacy Oath*;
> Did they not, next, compell the *Nation*,
> To take, and break the *Protestation*?
> To *swear*, and after to *recant*
> The *Solemn League and Covenant*?
> To take th'*Engagement*, and disclaim it,
> Enforc'd by those, who first did frame it?
> Did they not swear at first, to *fight*
> For the *King's Safety*, and His *Right*?
> And after march'd to find him out,
> And charg'd him home with *Horse* and *Foot*?[125]

Again he attacked, as others had done, but more memorably, the way in which the London mob had ignorantly and noisily supported the cry for reform of the Church—

> When *Tinkers* bawl'd aloud, to settle
> *Church Discipline*, for patching *Kettle*....
> The *Oyster-women* lock'd their Fish up,
> And trudg'd away to cry *No Bishop*....
> *Botchers* left old *Cloaths* in the lurch,
> And fell to turn and patch the *Church*.

> Some cried the *Covenant* instead
> Of *Pudding-pies* and *Ginger-bread*:
> And some for Brooms, old Boots and *Shooes*,
> Baul'd out to *purge* the *Commons House*:...
> A strange harmonious inclination
> Of all degrees to *Reformation*.[126]

He mocked too at another common butt of the Civil War satirists—the astrologers whose predictions obediently supplied the requirements of the dominant party and made the whole zodiac serve the Parliamentary cause. There had been Royalist astrologers whose predictions had been useful to the Cavaliers, but Butler passed them over. The Parliamentarian toadies alone were his target, those who:

> point-blank foretold
> Whats'er the close *Committee* would?
> Made *Mars* and *Saturn* for the *Cause*,
> The *Moon* for fundamental *Laws*?
> The *Ram*, and *Bull*, and *Goat* declare
> Against the Book of *Common Pray'r*?
> The *Scorpion* take the *Protestation*,
> The *Bear* engage for *Reformation*?
> Made all the *Royal Stars* recant,
> Compound, and take the *Covenant*.[127]

But though Butler picked up and developed themes familiar in the war his poem does not belong to the Civil War. It belongs to the aftermath and is morally much closer to the 'antigenius days' of which Alexander Brome had complained, to the years of emptiness and disillusion, than it is to the cheerfully abusive have-at-you mood of Denham,

Cleveland and the others in the early forties. The famous opening lines of *Hudibras* are significant:

> When *civil* fury first grew high,
> And men fell out they knew not why,
> When hard *Words*, *Jealousies* and *Fears*,
> Set Folks together by the Ears,
> And made them fight, like mad or drunk,
> For Dame *Religion* as for Punk,
> Whose honesty they all durst swear for,
> Though not a man of them knew wherefore....[128]

In 1662, these lines could be and were joyfully hailed as a trenchant and brilliantly satirical account of what had happened twenty years before. Would they have made any sense at all to the men and minds of 1642? Certainly neither Hampden nor Cromwell would have recognised the outbreak of the Civil War in those eight lines; but would King Charles I have done so? Would Falkland? What would the average honest Royalist and loyal churchman, in that earlier time, have made of the extraordinary reference to 'Dame Religion'? Butler's contemptuous abuse of the Puritans and the derision poured on Hudibras, ultimately reduce the whole conflict to absurdity.

Hudibras did not, of course, come within a hundred miles of any fighting for Dame Religion; his adventures were confined to contacts with a bear-warden, an astrologer and a rich widow whom he hoped to marry. If this was unfair to the Puritans, the Cavaliers as much as their opponents were dismissed in that contemptuous line: 'Men fell out they knew not why.' Butler could evidently see and admire nobility and singleness of purpose, but it was not until he added a third part to the poem fifteen years later that, in four unexpectedly quiet lines, he commemorated the silent, unrewarded older generation of Cavaliers:

> For loyalty is still the same
> Whether it win or lose the game
> True as the dial to the sun
> Altho' it be not shined upon.[129]

In general Butler saw the world without compassion and without admiration, denying to humanity the slightest spark of nobility. The satire on the cowardly hypocritical Roundhead, but also the implied satire on the whole war generation, made the poem instantly popular in 1662, with a generation who were bored with the ancient quarrel and glad to see the idealisms of their fathers reduced to this level.

The extraordinary verbal felicity of the poem, the ingenuity and wit of the rhymes, the quickness with which Butler catches and transfixes what are not only Puritan or Presbyterian failings but common human frailties, pretensions and self-deceptions, have made it a favourite source of quotations down to our own time. Lines like:

> Such as do build their Faith upon
> The holy Text of *Pike* and *Gun*;

> Decide all Controversies by
> Infallible *Artillery*;
> And prove their Doctrine Orthodox
> By Apostolick *Blows* and *Knocks*;[130]

—these were sure of popularity far outlasting the occasion for which they were written, because this kind of militant argument is a permanently recognisable feature in human society. So is the dyspeptic point of view that Butler associates by name with the Presbyterians, though he seems to have had other groups also in mind:

> A Sect, whose chief Devotion lies
> In odd perverse Antipathies;
> In falling out with that or this,
> And finding somewhat still amiss:
> More peevish, cross and splenetick
> Than Dog distract, or Monky sick.
> That with more care keep Holy-day
> The wrong, than others the right way:
> Compound for Sins they are inclin'd to;
> By damning those they have no mind to;
> Still so perverse and opposite,
> As if they worshipp'd God for spight.[131]

But these lines were not written, or at least they were not made public until it was safe to kick the Puritans. *Hudibras* became popular reading when the sectaries and Presbyterians were themselves oppressed by a vindictive persecution, and the Good Old Cause was being stifled in the blood of its martyrs; an age when turncoats and time-servers

were in the ascendant. For this reason I find
something ugly in *Hudibras*, that was not present
in the cruder, less brilliant, more combative,
Cavalier satires, the squibs of Denham, the lampoons of Cleveland, the anonymous scribblings
and songs of defiance, of which *Hudibras* is the last
descendant.

Against the ludicrous and contemptible figure of
Hudibras we ought to remember 'Michael and his
angels', the stern warriors of Wither's battle hymn;
we ought to remember how God was plainly seen—
by some at least—at Naseby fight; we ought to
remember those Joshuas and Gideons of the Civil
War, Oliver Cromwell, Thomas Harrison and others
who had felt the hand of the Almighty leading them,
and whose dissected and dishonoured bodies hung
on gibbets while Butler's angry derisive lines were
read and quoted by all the wits. Against those
'Apostolic blows and knocks' we must remember
the vibrant sincerity of Marvell's tribute to Cromwell:

> He first put arms into religion's hand
> And timorous conscience unto courage manned.

Neither the verbal warfare nor the deeper spiritual
and political conflict was yet over, though an interval of moral exhaustion had been reached. Butler
was no fighter like Cleveland, his friend and master;
he is the sneering voice of that interval.

Andrew Marvell, almost alone of those who had grieved in verse over Cromwell, had not turned his talents two years later to welcoming King Charles II; he watched the unfolding of events from his seat in Parliament as member for Hull, and would in due time, and in bitterness of spirit, carry the history of English satire a long step further.

V

SATIRE AND EULOGY

In the reign of Charles II political satire came of age. The Civil War and Commonwealth epochs had given rise to much political comment, chiefly from the defeated Cavaliers, which was wittily malicious, combative, stimulating to contemporaries, sometimes memorable. It was also often awkward and clumsy, and its writers fell into the fault which commonly besets those who use invective—that of dragging in too much. Those who wrote in secret, circulated their work anonymously, and were in danger from the government in power, naturally developed a reckless habit of mind—or had it by nature, or they would not have taken up the business of writing political satire. Recklessness does not go with that precision of aim that marks the best satire. The Cavalier satirists from 1640 to 1660 fired wildly and sometimes hit a target. The same wild firing is characteristic of the anti-Cavalier, anti-Court satire of Charles II's reign, but the target of an immoral Court, a corrupt government and a subservient Parliament was a large one, and bull's-eyes were frequently scored.

The satire of the seventeenth century only

achieves economy of expression and absolute certainty of direction with Dryden, and Dryden was not writing (like Marvell, the greatest satirist on the opposing side) from a position of danger. He was writing from a sheltered position in Court favour. He was after all Poet Laureate. If these external considerations are not the reason why *Absalom and Achitophel* outsoars all previous satire, neither are they altogether irrelevant. The facts here seem to contradict the frequently made assertion that men and parties in opposition necessarily produce the best satires.

The age of Charles II was rich also in political and Court verse of the official and complimentary kind, much of it pleasing, some of it exquisite in its elegance and grace.

King Charles II was crowned on a day of doubtful weather with what the modern cliché calls 'bright intervals'; Katherine Philips, the 'matchless Orinda', a poet whose breeding and style belonged to an earlier epoch, had a better word for it. Apollo, she wrote,

> check'd th' invading rains we fear'd,
> And in a bright parenthesis appear'd
> So that we knew not which look'd most content,
> The King, the people, or the firmament.[132]

The plaints of disappointed Cavaliers were heard in the ante-rooms of Whitehall and in many a straitened country house of the early 1660's, and the defeated Puritans, over whom Samuel Butler

uproariously triumphed in his *Hudibras*, mourned the
extinction of their hopes. But at Court, in the wider
circle of London, and among the majority of the
younger generation everywhere, the returned king
enjoyed for some years a warm personal popularity
and was, for a time at least, the centre of the reput-
able hopes and aspirations of his loyal subjects.
This was to prove no more than a 'bright parenthesis', but this temporary contentment was immediately reflected in the flattering words of poets
at, or near to, the Court. Their language, though
luscious enough, is less extravagant than the fantastic praise in which the doomed monarchy of
Charles I had been lauded. There was at first a
sustained attempt to praise the king as he really was,
not in terms of allegory. Dryden, on Coronation
Day, made the king's notorious good nature a part
of his theme, and added to it, quite truthfully, his
interest and skill in nautical matters, his pleasure in
and knowledge of sailing.

> Virtues unknown to these rough Northern climes
> From milder heav'ns you bring, without their crimes.
> Your calmnesse does no after storms provide
> Nor seeming patience mortal anger hide.
> When Empire first from families did spring,
> Then every Father govern'd as a King;
> But you that are a Sovereign Prince, allay
> Imperial pow'r with your paternal sway.
> From those great cares when ease your soul unbends,
> Your Pleasures are design'd to noble ends:

> Born to command the Mistress of the Seas,
> Your Thoughts themselves in that blue Empire please.
> Hither in Summer ev'nings you repair
> To take the fraischeur of the purer air....
> In stately frigats most delight you find,
> Where well-drawn Battels fire your martial mind.
> What to your cares we owe is learnt from hence,
> When ev'n your pleasures serve for our defence.[133]

Obsequious Waller overdoes it a little in the lines he published in 1664 in which he made the recent improvements in the laying out of St James's Park illustrate afresh the young king's pre-eminent virtues: first his skill at games—

> His manly posture, and his graceful mien,
> Vigour and youth, in all his motions seen;
> His shape so comely, and his limbs so strong,
> Confirm our hopes we shall obey him long.

The newly planted avenues of trees Waller compares to sacred groves where antique kings consulted wise men, and—

> Here Charles contrives the ordering of his states,
> Here he resolves his neighbouring princes' fates;
> What nation shall have peace, where war be made,
> Determined is in this oraculous shade....

He imagines the king seeing afar the roof of Westminster Hall, and contemplating the administration of justice:

> On which reflecting in his mighty mind,
> No private passion does indulgence find;
> The pleasures of his youth suspended are,
> And made a sacrifice to public care;

and concludes:

> A prince, on whom such different lights did smile,
> Born the divided world to reconcile!
> Whatever Heaven, or high extracted blood
> Could promise, or foretell, he will make good;
> Reform these nations, and improve them more,
> Than this fair park, from what it was before.[134]

Later the king's return and the impression he made would be somewhat differently described; and indeed Dryden and Waller with all this talk of yachting and landscape gardening had omitted a good deal in their account of Charles II that was immediately noticeable to his subjects, though they were not at first inclined to be censorious. An anonymous satirist, some years after, drew the king's first coming very differently:

> Of a tall Stature and of sable Hue;
> Much like the son of *Kish*, that lofty *Jew*:
> Twelve years compleat he suffer'd in Exile,
> And kept his Father's Asses all the while.
> At length by wonderful Impulse of Fate,
> The People call him home to help the State;
> And what is more, they send him Money too,
> And clothe him all, from Head to Foot, anew.
> Nor did he such small Favours then disdain,
> Who in his Thirtieth Year began his Reign:
> In a slasht Doublet then he came ashore,
> And dubb'd poor *Palmer*'s wife his royal Whore.
> Bishops and Deans, Peers, Pimps, and Knights he made,
> Things highly fitting for a Monarch's Trade;
> With Women, Wine and Viands of Delight,
> His jolly Vassals feast him Day and Night....[135]

Like most of the satires of the reign, this one circulated in manuscript and was freely but not accurately attributed to Marvell. It certainly comes as a shock after the compliments which welcomed the king's return. The contrast between the graceful hyperbole of courtly verse and the ferocious candour of satire was never more marked than in the reign of Charles II when courtly verse was at its most polished and fluent, satire at its most fluent and bitter.

The 'bright parenthesis' of the king's first coming did not last long. Murmuring against the frivolity and corruption of the Court and government began within a couple of years. By the middle 1660's, with a Dutch war going badly, with unpaid mutinous seamen making the streets dangerous, or deserting to the enemy, with the appalling ravage of the Plague and the spectacular disaster of the Great Fire, there was much discontent, popular criticism and talk of judgments on the Court and kingdom. John Dryden, in his *Annus Mirabilis* which describes the events of the year 1666, does much more than merely narrate them. His poem is an answer, by a supporter of the Court, to the criticisms and prophecies of its enemies. He presents the Plague and Fire not as judgments but as trials of endurance merely; he describes with considerable justice the valiant conduct of the naval commanders, and he praises the development of science and increase of trade. There are some pleasing verses on the improvements in navigation from better astronomical observation.

> Instructed ships shall sail to quick Commerce;
> By which remotest Regions are alli'd:
> Which makes one City of the Universe,
> Where some may gain, and all may be suppli'd.

> Then, we upon our Globe's last verge shall go,
> And view the Ocean leaning on the sky:
> From thence our rolling Neighbours we shall know,
> And on the Lunar world securely pry.

There follows an apostrophe to the Royal Society as the source of all this new and useful knowledge:

> This I foretel from your auspicious care,
> Who great in search of God and Nature grow:
> Who best your wise Creator's praise declare,
> Since best to praise his works is best to know.

> O truly Royal! who behold the Law,
> And rule of beings in your Maker's mind,
> And thence, like Limbecks, rich Ideas draw
> To fit the levell'd use of humane kind.

There is something really noble in this luminous prophecy of a world united by better navigation, enlightened by science, enriched by trade; Dryden concludes with a prophetic tribute to London, risen from the ashes of the Great Fire, and become the mart and mistress of the world:

> Now, like a Maiden Queen, she will behold,
> From her high Turrets, hourly Sutors come:
> The East with Incense, and the West with Gold,
> Will stand, like Suppliants, to receive her doom.

> The silver *Thames*, her own domestick Floud,
> Shall bear her Vessels, like a sweeping Train;
> And often wind (as of his Mistress proud)
> With longing eyes to see her face again.

Dryden had not a very original or penetrating mind. This vision was not of his own invention, but was the ideal prospect that men of understanding saw unfolding before them in the middle years of the century. It has—to us—less pleasing aspects, because to an active and intelligent people the first necessity seemed the establishment of maritime and mercantile supremacy.

> But first the toils of war we must endure
> And from th' injurious Dutch redeem the seas.... [136]

The aggressive sentiment is expressed without any compunction and reflects the general feeling of the time. The critics of the government objected not to the war but to what it cost and to the incompetence (as they thought) of its prosecution. It was not until some years later that a shift of public opinion made the Dutch allies and the French the national enemy.

Dryden's *Annus Mirabilis* was read with pleasure and approval by Samuel Pepys, and quite apart from its often great beauties of narrative and descriptive verse, it was a convincing tract for the times.

The same cannot be said of Waller's helpful but inept attempt to glorify the Dutch war in a poem called *Instructions to a Painter for the drawing of the*

*posture and progress of his Majesty's forces at sea under
the command of His Highness Royal*—the Duke of York,
the King's brother. Waller spreads flattery like
butter; it is the very best butter, but that hardly
justifies it. Hear him instruct his painter how to
paint the Duke of York—

> Let thy bold pencil hope and courage spread
> Through the whole navy, by that hero led;
> Make all appear, where such a Prince is by,
> Resolved to conquer, or resolved to die.
> With his extraction, and his glorious mind,
> Make the proud sails swell more than with the wind;
> Preventing cannon, make his louder fame
> Check the Batavians, and their fury tame....
> Make him bestride the ocean, and mankind
> Ask his consent to use the sea and wind....

The Duke of York was a competent commander
and a brave man, and it was not his fault that, after
the Battle of Lowestoft, which takes up most of
Waller's poem, the discomfited Dutch fleet was
allowed to escape owing to a mistaken order to stop
the pursuit, given while the Duke was asleep.
Popular opinion is apt to be unjust in such matters
and though no one can seriously blame the Duke for
needing a little rest, being asleep when a critical
mistake is made is something that only an excep-
tionally popular and successful commander will ever
be allowed to live down.

Waller's fulsome poem touched off the angry wit
of those who criticised the conduct of the war.

Instructions to a Painter or *Directions* or *Advice* became within a few months a recognised formula for attacks on the government. The stillness which had fallen on political satire since the Restoration was suddenly broken; broadsheets and manuscripts multiplied, some without authors, some with famous names spuriously added. Confusions of authorship cannot, over a great part of this period, be disentangled. Four of these *Directions to a Painter* appeared within about a year of Waller's poem, attacking the Court and the Duke with extraordinary venom, justly mocking the pretentiousness of Waller's praise. Of the death of the newly created Lord Falmouth, a favourite courtier, killed while standing beside the Duke of York, Waller has this:

> On such a theatre as this to die,
> For such a cause, with such a witness by!
> Who would not thus a sacrifice be made,
> To have his blood on such an altar laid?[137]

This in the satirical rejoinder becomes:

> Such was his rise, such was his fall, unpraised,
> A chance shot sooner took him than chance raised,
> His shattered head the fearless Duke distains—
> And gave the last, first proof that he had brains.[138]

In an apostrophe to the king, the same satirist expresses devoted loyalty but urges him to look to the corruptions of his Court, in an unpleasant but apt metaphor:

> What boots it that thy Light doth gild our Days
> And we lie basking in thy milder Rays,

While Swarms of Insects, from thy Warmth begun
Our Land devour and intercept our Sun?[139]

Several of these *Directions to a Painter* were assigned
to Sir John Denham but, although this once witty
and now ageing Cavalier poet had good reason to
hate the Court because the Duke of York had
seduced his young wife, his griefs did not take a
literary form. Instead, he went out of his mind and
informed King Charles II that he was the Holy
Ghost. His name was attached to these vituperative
satires because, after John Cleveland, he had been
the best known satirical writer among the old
Cavaliers. Cleveland had been dead for some years,
and those seeking credit for their new productions
would naturally seize on Denham's name now that
Cleveland was gone. The first use of mock *Directions
to a Painter* was followed in the autumn of 1667 by
Last Instructions to a Painter (not that they were to
be the last, for the *genre* went on until the end of the
century) which was by far the most telling yet to be
published and was from the hand of Marvell.
Beginning with a bitter sneer at the mismanagement
of the war:

Can'st thou paint without Colours? Then 'tis right:
For so we too without a Fleet can fight....

the writer moves on to attack with obscene ferocity
the Court, the king's ministers, the venal and incompetent members of Parliament, the delays and

disorders that led to the final disaster when the
Dutch sailed up the Medway:

> There our sick Ships unrigg'd in Summer lay,
> Like molting Fowl, a weak and easie Prey....

He describes the veteran General Monk striving to
hold back the enemy, hampered at every turn by
silly courtiers and mutinous seamen:

> Our feather'd *Gallants*, which came down that day
> To be Spectators safe of the *new Play*,
> Leave him alone when first they hear the Gun;
> (*Cornbury* the fleetest) and to *London* run.
> Our Seamen, whom no Dangers shape could fright,
> Unpaid, refuse to mount our Ships for Spight:

and so the valiant old commander

> ...finds, wheresoe're he Succour might expect,
> Confusion, folly, treach'ry, fear, neglect.

From this scene of tumult and shame Marvell passes
to Parliament again, to the excuses and recriminations, the patching up of peace, and he reaches at
length the sinister climax of the poem—

> Paint last the King, and a dead shade of Night,
> Only dispers'd by a weak Taper's light....
> There, as in the calm Horrour all alone,
> He wakes and Muses of th' uneasie Throne....

To the king in this anxious mood appears a dis-
hevelled and distressed virgin, a figure symbolic (the
poet indicates) perhaps of endangered and woe-
begone England, perhaps of shattered peace; but

the king's behaviour to the symbolic visitant is that
of the gallant gentleman we know he was:

> The Object strange in him no Terrour mov'd,
> He wonder'd first, then pity'd, then he lov'd;
> And with kind hand does the coy Vision press,
> Whose Beauty greater seem'd by her distress:
> But soon shrunk back, chil'd with her Touch so cold,
> And th' airy Picture vanisht from his hold.... [140]

It is only after the illusion has fled that he begins to
muse on who she can have been; there is a macabre
humour in this short scene, after which the more
conventional apparition of the murdered Charles I,
with which the poem ends, is an anticlimax. The
idea of Charles II attempting to console a vision of
his distressed country by squeezing her hand is a
biting comment on his failure to appreciate the
serious nature of government.

Whether the comment is just or not, the poem has
a formidable power. Andrew Marvell was in the
later 1660's and 1670's responsible for the most
excoriating satirical attacks on the Court and the
royal government. As a member of Parliament he
saw how the exhausted desire for peace after the
Civil Wars decayed quickly into an easy-going
corruption; he was a frequent witness of the extreme
venality and frequently unseemly behaviour of the
members of the Cavalier Parliament. Everyone from
contemptuous courtiers downwards to ballad-
reading apprentices thought poorly of this Parlia-

ment which is lampooned alike in sophisticated
satire and popular doggerel.

> The *Senate*, which should headstrong Princes stay,
> Lets loose the Reins, and gives the Realm away;
> With lavish Hands they constant Tributes give,
> And annual Stipends for their Guilt receive.
> Corrupt with Gold, they Wives and Daughters bring
> To the Black idol for an Offering.... [141]

The lines are among many foisted on to Marvell by
contemporaries.

When the king in 1668 prorogued Parliament, the
members were represented in a popular ballad as
complaining

> Have we our country plagued and trust betrayed
> Given polls and subsidies and royal aid,
> Hearth money imposts on the lawyers fees,
> Ruined all trades, tormented all degrees
> Crushed the poor phanaticks, broke through all laws
> Of Magna Charta and the good old Cause
> > To be thus fooled at last? [142]

Eight years later Rochester, at once a brilliant figure
at Court and a savage critic of the very vices he
practised, describes the way in which 'chaste, pious,
prudent Charles the Second' managed his House of
Commons:

> A Parliament of Knaves and Sots,
> Members by name you must not mention,
> He keeps in Pay, and buys their Votes,
> Here with a Place, there with a Pension,
> When to give Money he can't collogue 'em
> He does with Scorn prorogue, prorogue 'em.

> But they long since by too much giving
> Undid, betray'd and sold the Nation;
> Making their Membership a Living
> Better than ere was Sequestration.[143]

With the same unanimity the satirists attacked the Court; its frivolity and immorality was an obvious target and comes up repeatedly in the satire of the later 1660's and early 1670's. The statue of King Charles I at the head of Whitehall is depicted melting with grief because he has to contemplate 'such a prodigal Court and a son'. In another lampoon his horse, endowed with speech, laments the elevation of the king's mistresses and their children:

> The Misses take place, and advanc'd to be Dutchess,
> With Pomp great as Queens in their Coach and six Horses:
> Their Bastards made Dukes, Earls, Viscounts, and Lords,
> And all the high Titles that Honour affords.[144]

There is not the slighest attempt to spare the king personally in these satires. When the king was given the freedom of the City of London in 1674 a lampoon, doubtfully ascribed to Marvell, describes Charles's career in terms of a dissolute and idle apprentice:

> He spends all his days in running to Plays,
> When he should in the Shop be poring;
> And he wasts all his Nights in his constant Delights,
> Of Revelling, Drinking and Whoring.
>
> Throughout *Lombard-street*, each Man he did meet,
> He would run on the *Score* and *Borrow*;
> When they ask'd for their own, he was broke and gone,
> And his Creditors left to sorrow.

Though oft bound to the Peace, yet he never would cease
To vex his poor Neighbours with Quarrels;
And when he was beat, he still made his Retreat
To his Clevelands, his Nells, and his Carwells.[145]

In another lampoon the king is represented as
saying:

I'll have a religion all of my own
Whether Popish or Protestant shall not be known,
And if it prove troublesome I will have none....
I'll wholly abandon all public affairs,
And pass all my time with buffoons and players,
And saunter to Nelly, when I should be at prayers.[146]

Rochester, in some lines beginning—with seeming
mildness—

There reigns and long may he reign and thrive
The easiest Prince and best bred Man alive[147]

delivers a personal attack on the king of such
staggering insolence that he had to leave Court for
a time. In any other reign he would have had to
leave it forever.

But, as in the first half of the century, it is ultimately at the foreign policy of the Crown that
criticism is directed with most ferocity. With the
decline of Spain and the emergence of the France
of Louis XIV as the dominant power in Europe,
popular fears, once so vocal against Spain, now
centred—not without reason—on France. Since
Louis XIV had taken over together with leadership
in European politics, the Spanish claim to crusade

for the Catholic Church, that ancient pattern of public prejudice which linked the national enemy with the Roman Catholic religion was exactly reproduced once more.

It is interesting, in this context, to compare Oldham's satire on the Jesuits written at this time, which describes a session of their distinguished dead in Hell plotting the destruction of English Protestantism, with Phineas Fletcher's treatment of exactly the same subject in *The Apollyonists* fifty years earlier. Comparisons of this kind bring out with uncanny effect the dominant politico-religious preoccupations which, with a few changes in *dramatis personae*, persisted through the reigns of the first four Stuarts. As with King James I and King Charles I, so again with King Charles II, it was this constant flying in the face of widespread and deeply-rooted convictions among his people which destroyed public confidence and undermined the throne.

King James I and even more King Charles I had pursued a pro-Spanish policy abroad, linked by King Charles with a pro-Catholic policy at home. King Charles II pursued a pro-French policy abroad, even more closely linked with a pro-Catholic policy at home, and relied on French subsidies to make him independent of criticism, just as his father had depended, to the same end, on Spanish silver. It was also of course extremely noticeable that the Stuarts aligned themselves unfailingly with the power in Europe which at that moment most effectively embodied the practice of monarchical supremacy.

A satire which circulated about 1675 under the name of *Britannia and Raleigh* is particularly interesting in this respect because it openly links the plaints of Britannia against Charles II's French policy with the name of Sir Walter Raleigh who was popularly remembered as the most illustrious victim of the Spanish policy of King James I. Britannia, creeping away 'whilst the lewd Court in drunken slumber lies', pours out her woes to the shade of Raleigh:

> A Colony of *French* possess the Court;
> *Pimps, priests, buffoons,* in Privy Chamber sport.
> Such slimy Monsters ne'er approach'd a Throne,
> Since Pharaoh's days, nor so defil'd a Crown.
> In sacred Ear Tyrannic Arts they croak,
> Pervert his Mind, and good Intention choak;
> Tell him of Golden *Indies*, Fairy Lands,
> *Leviathan,* and absolute Commands.
> Thus, Fairy-like, the King they steal away
> And in his room a Changeling *Lewis* lay.

She goes on to make particular complaint of the ascendancy of Louise de Kéroualle, commonly called 'Madam Carwell':

> Frequent Addresses to my *Charles* I send,
> And my sad State did to his Care commend,
> But his fair Soul transform'd by that *French* Dame,
> Had lost a Sense of Honour, Justice, Fame....
> Lull'd in Security, rolling in Lust,
> Resigns his Crown to Angel Carwell's Trust....

Raleigh very loyally tries to persuade Britannia to make one more effort to reach the king's better nature but she interrupts:

> *Raleigh*, no more; for long in vain I've try'd,
> The *Stuart* from the Tyrant to divide....[148]

and goes on to suggest quite openly the dethronement of the Stuart race and the establishment of an English republic on the Venetian model. In this satire, criticism of the morals of the Court has hardened into a reckless political attack. The effect is sharper still in another lampoon of the same date, probably authentic Marvell, *A Dialogue between two Horses*—the horses are 'the stately brass stallion and the white marble steed' from the respective statues of Charles I in Whitehall and of Charles II recently put up in the Stocks market. Of this latter Marvell had already written:

> But a market, they say, does suit the king well,
> Who the Parliament buys and revenues does sell,
> And others to make the similitude hold
> Say his Majesty himself is bought too and sold.[149]

In the *Dialogue between the two Horses*: the creatures meet

> When both Kings were weary of sitting all day,
> Were stolen off *Incognito* each his own way.

Later on we learn from the horses, that Charles I has gone to meet the shade of Archbishop Laud, and Charles II to cuckold a merchant in the City.

After the usual angry denunciations of the Court, and of the corruption of ministers, the horses condemn the venal Parliament:

> Four Knights and a Knave, who were Publicans made,
> For selling their Consciences were Liberally paid.
> Yet baser the souls of those low-pricéd Sinners
> Who vote with the Court for drink and for Dinners.

After some brisk interchanges of this kind, the two horses fall to comparing their riders. The steed of Charles II abuses Charles I:

> The Priest-ridden King turn'd desperate Fighter
> For the *Surplice*, *Lawn-sleeves*, the *Cross* and the *Mitre*;
> Till at last on a *Scaffold* he was left in the lurch
> By Knaves, who cry'd up themselves for the Church.

Charles I's horse makes rather a lame effort to defend his master, but his companion cuts him short:

> Tho' the Father and Sonne be different Rodds,
> Between the two Scourges wee find little odds.
> Both Infamous Stand in three Kingdoms Votes,
> This for picking our Pocketts, that for cutting our Throats.

Even more outspokenly he adds that if we must have a tyrant: I am for old *Noll*

> Tho' his government did a Tyrants resemble,
> He made England great, and its Enemies tremble.

Charles I's horse at this throws discretion to the winds and shouts—or perhaps neighs—

> A Tudor a Tudor! wee've had Stuarts enough;
> None ever Reign'd like old Besse in the Ruffe.[150]

This satire concentrates almost entirely on national pride and national humiliation, crying up the obvious moments of military and maritime achievement. But there was also a growing political opposition, a resuscitation of political ideas which fear had held in abeyance, and increasingly outspoken criticism of the theory of Divine Right which the conduct of the reigning king was seen to bring into disrepute. Rochester, writing in 1676, seemed to direct his wrath on this score against the king of France, but it is clear that a great part of this impassioned attack on Divine Right, in his *History of Insipids,* is intended by implication for Charles II:

> That false rapacious Wolf of France,
> The Scourge of Europe and its Curse
> Who at his Subjects' cry does Dance,
> And study how to make them worse,
> To say such Kings, Lord, rule by thee,
> Were most prodigious Blasphemy....
>
> Such Kings, curst be their Power and Name
> Let all the World henceforth abhor 'em
> Monsters which Knaves Sacred proclaim
> And then like Slaves fall down before 'em
> What can there be in Kings Divine?
> The most are Wolves, Goats, Sheep, or Swine.[151]

It is a vigorous plea against tyranny. But in spite of such fierce outbursts, the opposition under Charles II compares very poorly, in all its moral qualities, with the opposition under Charles I. This second half of the century has many villains, but few heroes. The king's government was corrupt and his lackeying to France was humiliating and not in the best interest of his people. But his opponents did not elevate the tone of politics by stimulating the hideous business of the Popish Plot and by setting up the king's illegitimate son, Monmouth, as a claimant to the throne. A din of popular and satirical comment mostly from unidentified writers resounded in the terrible years from 1678 to 1681 during the frenzied counter-attack on the Catholics, when the Whigs under Shaftesbury's leadership irresponsibly aroused the worst instincts of the rabble. Among many I quote a clumsy but popular street ballad, chiefly because it reveals in its ingenuousness the way in which unrelated matters can be linked together in popular opinion to stimulate the fires of hate and unreason: it is called *A Looking Glass for all true Protestants*, and its only saving grace is a refrain which at least suggests a certain consciousness of sin. The discovery of the wholly imaginary Popish Plot is ascribed to divine intervention:

> But our good God with his All-seeing Eye,
> He found them out and quickly them did spye:
> He dasht them all to pieces in a trice,
> Let's love the truth, and all believe in Christ.

And now for the economic causes—

> Oh! what a broyl amongst us has been made,
> These Popish Jesuits they have spoyl'd our trade:

> Which makes the Nation for to suffer sore,
> And very hard it goes amongst the Poor.
> *Let's not despair, but call to God on high*
> And repent our sins, and to him for mercy cry.[152]

This popular association of repentance and amendment with deliverance from the Popish Plot appears also in much more sophisticated verses. *Sir Edmundbury Godfrey's Ghost* is an example of this. The murder of this elderly and respected magistrate—as it was alleged, by the Papists—had started the whole Plot scare. The author, evidently a practised writer, borrowed his scene-setting from Marvell's *Last Instructions to a Painter*; the king is in his bedroom, not alone this time but with his faithful attendant Chiffinch:

> It happened in the Twilight of the Day,
> As *England*'s Monarch in his Closet lay,
> And *Chiffinch* step'd to fetch the female Prey;
> The bloody Shape of *Godfrey* did appear,
> And in sad Vocal Sounds these things declare—

Godfrey's ghost divides his time between a denunciation of the Roman Catholics and a reproachful entreaty to the king to reform his Court, and concludes with a condemnation of the doctrine of Divine Right and of those Anglicans who uphold it:

> Trust not in Prelates false Divinity,
> Who wrong their Prince, and shame their Deity;
> Making their God so partial in their Cause,
> Exempting King's alone from human Laws.
> These lying Oracles, they did infuse
> Of old, and did your *Martyr'd Sire* abuse.

After the grisly apparition has withdrawn, the writer concludes with a quatrain that faintly echoes Marvell's much more bold and subtle use of the same theme—

> The Ghost spake thus, groaned thrice, and said no more;
> Straight in came *Chiffinch*, hand in hand, with Whore;
> The King, tho' much concerned twixt Joy and Fear,
> Starts from the Couch, and bids the Dame draw near.[153]

The great majority of the satirists of this reign had hitherto been against the Court and government, and had gone unanswered. Marvell died in 1678, and although there were others writing, the themes were growing stale; there is a great deal of repetition, and some working-over of older poems to insert more modern allusions, a common practice which increases the difficulty of identifying the writers. From 1679 to 1682 the king's resistance to the bill for excluding his brother the Roman Catholic Duke of York from the succession, and the manipulation of the mob by Shaftesbury, brought the country within distance of a new Civil War. As the danger abated the inevitable reaction followed. Outside London, with its unreliable and highly excitable populace, the majority, though staunch for Protestantism, were more afraid of a new Civil War than of the accession of the king's Catholic brother. The king's firmness on the Exclusion Bill had its reward, as Dryden was approvingly to point out:

> Not Faction, when it shook thy Regal Seat,
> Not senates, insolently loud,

(Those Ecchoes of a thoughtless Croud,)
Not Foreign or Domestick Treachery,
Could Warp thy Soul to their Unjust Decree.
So much thy Foes thy manly Mind mistook,
Who judgd it by the Mildness of thy look:
Like a well-temper'd Sword, it bent at will;
But kept the Native toughness of the Steel.[154]

These lines were not written until after the king's death in 1685. But on the turn of the tide, after the dissolution of the king's last Parliament, in Oxford in the spring of 1681 and before the trial of Shaftesbury in November of that year, Dryden wrote the most famous satire of the century *Absalom and Achitophel*, that excoriating exposure of the Whig leaders under a transparent biblical disguise.

The poem was enormously successful—it could hardly have been anything else. It combines the daring, the vituperation and the wit which men had learnt to look for in satires over the last forty years, with a smoothness and easy skill far beyond anything yet seen. But whether it was politically influential or not is quite another question; it was, writes a modern editor, 'evidently meant to appear at the psychological moment for exciting public sentiment against Shaftesbury'.[155] It came out exactly a week in advance of Shaftesbury's appearance before the Middlesex Grand Jury on a charge of high treason, which seems to allow rather little time for its full impact to be felt, given the small numbers printed and the less advanced organs of salesmanship and publicity known in those days. Whatever the effect of the poem, the Grand Jury refused to find a true bill against Shaftesbury.

Far more important than the immediate impact of *Absalom and Achitophel* was its long term effect on the reputation of those whom Dryden attacked. He himself, in one of his typically suave and gentlemanly introductions, declares that 'the true end of satire is the amendment of the vices by correction. And he who writes honestly is no more an enemy to the offender than the physician to the patient, when he prescribes harsh remedies to an inveterate disease.'[155] In spite of these moderate words, it is difficult to imagine that Dryden, in describing Shaftesbury's Cromwellian youth, really felt anything but the desire to wound his enemy and to make him an object of hatred and contempt:

> A Vermin, wriggling in th' Usurper's ear,
> Bart'ring his venal wit for sums of gold
> He cast himself into the Saint-like mould;
> Groan'd, sigh'd and pray'd, while Godliness was gain,
> The lowest Bag-pipe of the squeaking train....[156]

This does not sound like a curative prescription; it sounds like what it is: a fatal dose to an enemy's reputation. Other satires, most satires indeed, make their impact immediately or not at all; Dryden fixed the portraits of his victims to last. In scope and number the satires written *against* the Court and its policies in this epoch are far more extensive than

Dryden's work; but they are read only by specialists in the period. A full knowledge of even Marvell's political verse is not an essential part of the equipment of every educated man. But not to be familiar with *Absalom and Achitophel* is not to be educated, and the reputations of Shaftesbury and of Buckingham (Achitophel and Zimri, the two characters in the poem most often quoted) have never fully recovered from it.

I do not, however, wish to dwell on these too well known passages; certain other aspects of this famous poem at the moment concern me more because they throw light on the general Tory reaction of which Dryden's satire was rather a first-fruit than a cause. He begins his biblical tale with the obvious identification of Charles II with David; and he makes this in itself an ingenious apologia for the king. The constant association of England with Israel—with the Chosen People—was a well-known Puritan habit of mind. Dryden is therefore adopting the very language and way of thought of those who had most keenly objected to the Court's immorality. But he turns this Puritan-biblical trick inside out; he makes it serve not for a condemnation, but for a justification of the lusty king.

> In pious Times, e'r Priest-Craft did begin,
> Before *Polygamy* was made a sin;
> When Man, on many, multiplied his kind,
> E'r one to one was, cursedly, confin'd:

> When Nature prompted, and no Law deni'd
> Promiscuous Use of Concubine and Bride;
> Then, *Israel*'s Monarch, after Heaven's own heart,
> His vigorous warmth did, variously, impart
> To Wives and Slaves: and, wide as his Command,
> Scatter'd his Maker's Image thro' the Land.[157]

Special pleading it may be, but it is a refreshing change after all that snarling and cursing about Carwells and Nellys, bastards and whores, and has the odd effect of making King Charles II's Court seem a wholesome patriarchal society.

A few lines later, keeping up the English–Jewish identification, Dryden gives us one of the key-passages of the satire, his comment on the English people of his time:

> The *Jews*, a Headstrong, Moody, Murm'ring race,
> As ever tri'd th' extent and stretch of grace;
> God's pampered People, whom, debauch'd with ease,
> No King could govern, nor no God could please;
> (Gods they had tri'd of every shape and size,
> That God-smiths could produce, or Priests devise:)
> These *Adam*-wits, too fortunately free,
> Began to dream they wanted liberty;
> And when no rule, no president, was found
> Of Men, by Laws less circumscrib'd and bound,
> They led their wild desires to Woods and Caves,
> And thought that all but Savages were Slaves.[158]

Leaving aside this sidelong shot at current political theories about noble savages, this is the statement of a man who remembers the excesses of the sects and the disorders of the Civil War, who sees how fatally easy it is to kindle into flame a 'Headstrong,

Moody, Murm'ring race'—a one-sided but not un-
true description of the seventeenth-century English
—and knows how difficult it will be to put out the
fire once kindled. Dryden hated and feared the
questioning, the fanaticism, the demands for liberty
which could lead to civil war, and in that un-
adventurous but not unworthy spirit he exactly
reflected the country-wide reaction which enabled
Charles II to overthrow the Whigs. Dryden also
reflected the contempt and suspicion into which the
conduct of Shaftesbury and his following in the
preceding years had brought such words as 'liberty'
and 'patriotism': thus Achitophel 'usurped a
patriot's all atoning name'; thus David describes his
son Absalom as—

> Gull'd with a Patriot's name, whose Modern sense
> Is one that woud by Law supplant his Prince:
> The People's Brave, the Politician's Tool;
> Never was Patriot yet, but was a Fool.[159]

Dryden brings up again all the old charges against
the opposers of Prerogative power, their lust for
power, their itch for profit, describing the whole
struggle between the Stuarts and their Parliaments
as the encroachment of selfish, ambitious men with
no interest to serve except their own: thus Achitophel calculates the bargaining powers of Parliament against the Crown:

> Tis true, he grants the People all they crave;
> And more perhaps than Subjects ought to have:

> Let him give on till he can give no more,
> The thrifty Sanhedrin shall keep him poor:
> And every shekle which he can receive,
> Shall cost a Limb of his Prerogative.
> To ply him with new Plots, shall be my care;
> Or plunge him deep in some Expensive War;
> Which, when his Treasure can no more supply,
> He must, with the Remains of Kingship, buy.[160]

Dryden uses the same contemptuous tone to describe the various types of Protestants who had joined in the outcry for the Exclusion Bill, neatly dismissing the destructive folly of fanatics, lingering with more critical distaste over those who had taken over from their fathers the Protestant religion, the spoils of the Church and all the prejudices that went with both:

> A numerous host of dreaming saints succeed,
> Of the true old enthusiastic breed:
> 'Gain'st form and order they their power employ,
> Nothing to build, and all things to destroy.
> But far more numerous was the herd of such,
> Who think too little, and who talk too much.
> These, out of mere instinct, they knew not why,
> Ador'd their father's God, and Property;
> And, by the same blind benefit of Fate,
> The Devil and the Jebusite did hate.[161]

And he never loses an opportunity of linking the idea of intolerant Protestantism with that of commercial gain—as for instance in the character of Shimei, Slingsby Bethel, the Whig sheriff of London:

Shimei, whose Youth did early Promise bring
Of Zeal to God, and Hatred to his King;
Did wisely from Expensive Sins refrain,
And never broke the Sabbath, but for Gain....[162]

The attack is deadly because it pervades the entire poem; there is none of that shifting about from one angry idea to another which makes even Marvell's satire, and certainly all the others, by comparison jerky and awkward. Dryden sincerely and eloquently preaches that all zealots and reformers are either fools or knaves, and elevates almost to a prophetic strain the cry of the temperate conservative, saying *Let well enough, alone*:

What prudent man a settled throne would shake?...
If ancient fabrics nod and threat to fall,
To patch the flaws and buttress up the wall
Thus far 'tis duty: but here fix the mark
For all beyond, it is to touch the ark.
To change foundations, cast the frame anew
Is work for rebels who base ends pursue
At once divine and human laws control
And mend the parts by ruin of the whole,
The tampering world is subject to this curse
To physic their disease into a worse.[163]

It is a timorous doctrine, but against the stormy background of 1681 a timely one. The reaction defeated the Whigs; the Duke of York, who had been forced into exile, was able to come home and until the end of the reign the lampoons and the ballads alike reflect the revulsion of opinion in the king's favour. Take for instance *A Health to the Royal Family* or the *Tories Delight*.

> He's no Tory baulks his wine
> let sneaking Whigs make faces,
> Who'd pull the King and Bishops down
> that they might have their places
> Here's to the Duke and Dutches healths
> wishing them long to live,
> And to all those that wish their fall
> their dues may Tyburn give.[164]

This ballad goes on to include the Duke of York's Protestant daughter, the Princess of Orange, and her husband in the toast, and to wish them 'health and wealth, peace, plenty and delight' and the birth of an heir as soon as possible. In fact it expresses devoted loyalty to the royal family provided there is a Protestant succession not too far off. The return of the Duke of York was welcomed in the confident hope that his wife would have no children to bar the succession of his Protestant daughter. A Roman Catholic king could be endured for the sake of peace, provided he did not start a Catholic dynasty.

The delightful poetry of compliment which had flowed so freely at the beginning of the reign had diminished to a mere trickle, an occasional congratulatory verse, during the middle years. Now at the end, it welled up again. Dryden welcomed home the Duchess of York with some very pretty variations on well-worn themes:

> But now the illustrious Nymph, return'd again,
> Brings every Grace triumphant in her Train:
> The wandering Nereids, though they rais'd no storm,
> Foreslow'd her Passage, to behold her Form....
> Far from her Sight flew Faction, Strife and Pride,
> And Envy did but look on her, and died....
> For her the weeping Heavens become serene,
> For her the Ground is clad in cheerful green,
> For her the Nightingales are taught to sing,
> And Nature has for her delay'd the Spring.

And finally the triumph of the Tories—

> Distemper'd Zeal, Sedition, canker'd Hate
> No more shall vex the Church and tear the State;
> No more shall Faction civil Discords move,
> Or only Discords of too tender love:...
> Discord that only this Dispute shall bring,
> Who best shall love the Duke and serve the King.[165]

Thomas Flatman in the words of his *Song before the King on New Years Day 1683* seems half the time to be deliberately uncertain whether he is talking of Charles II or of God:

> Rise, mighty Monarch, and ascend the Throne,
> 'Tis yet, once more your own,
> For Lucifer and all his legions are o'erthrown....[166]

This would appear in the context to refer to the discomfiture of Shaftesbury and the Whigs; Flatman had, before Dr Johnson, decided that the Devil was the first Whig.

In 1685 Dryden, in *Threnodia Augustalis*, his poem on the king's death, celebrated his virtues with more poetic assurance and more knowledge than he had been able to bring to his *Astraea Redux* in 1660 on the king's restoration; it contains a charming passage on the encouragement, verbal rather than financial, that the king had given to poets.

> Th' officious Muses came along,
> A gay Harmonious Quire, like Angels ever Young;...
> Even *they* cou'd thrive in his Auspicious reign;
> And such a plenteous Crop they bore,
> Of purest and well winow'd Grain
> As Britain never knew before.
> Tho' little was their Hire, and light their Gain,
> Yet somewhat to their share he threw;
> Fed from his hand, they sung and flew,
> Like Birds of Paradise that liv'd on morning dew.[167]

It is a charming fantasy, the poets like the birds in the ornamental walks in St James's Park, fed by the sauntering King; but not very well fed. There at least a hard unhappy reality breaks in. But this state poem, like nearly all that Dryden wrote in the genre, keeps fairly close to the facts, ennobling them as he does the character of the king and his brother, but not altogether losing sight of the reality. His lines on Charles's management of the Exclusion Bill crisis, which I quoted a few pages back, are a typical example. Within the poetic conventions, Dryden gives a recognisable account of what happened.

The same cannot be said of the praises showered on the dead king by Thomas Flatman:

> Our land (like Eden) flourish'd in his time,
> Defended by an Angel's Sword,
> A terror 'twas to those abroad,
> But all was Paradise to those within.[168]

Yet in his hollow, inflated manner Flatman picked up ideas that had been recurrent in the political poetry of the century; his lines are an insipid echo of the young Marvell's lament for the peaceful England of Charles I:

> Thou Paradise of four seas
> Which Heaven planted us to please.

The Court poets of King Charles I fifty years before—Carew, Townshend, Cartwright—had in their exalted praise of him made more outrageous claims than Flatman did, and far more outrageous claims than Dryden. Yet we feel a greater sympathy for them, a greater willingness to suspend disbelief, relax, and accept the fantasy world where the king and queen are stars of Heaven, and the planets revolve about the Court. The difference, which I shall consider at greater length later on, is not merely that the earlier poetry has greater freshness and a wider imaginative range; it was written in a different atmosphere. They did not know in the 1630's what lay ahead of them. In the 1680's they had experience and memory of civil war and mob rule; they had no excuse for not knowing the political possibilities before them. Were they consciously disguising fears, deliberately masking what was dangerous, squalid and uneasy in the political situation? When Aurelian Townshend called in the halcyon bird of peace as an emblem for King Charles I, we, his modern readers, are aware of tragic-ironic undertones of which he knew and guessed nothing. When Thomas Flatman, fifty years later, hailed King James II—'Dread Prince whom all the world admires and fears'—with a reference to the same overworked bird, we feel that he ought to know better, and respond with cynicism. When Court poets invoke the halcyon, revolution is round the corner.

VI

CONCLUSION

The accession and coronation of King James II was greeted with some popular as well as official enthusiasm. There was no cynical intention in the closing stanza of Dryden's elegy on the late King Charles, in which he prayed that God would inspire Parliament to give generous support to the new king's policies:

> Let them, with glad amazement, look
> On what their happiness may be:
> Let them not still be obstinately blind,
> Still to divert the Good thou hast design'd,
> Or with Malignant penury,
> To sterve the Royal vertues of his Mind.
> Faith is a Christian's and a Subject's Test,
> O give them to believe, and they are surely blest!
> They do; and, with a distant view, I see
> Th' amended Vows of English Loyalty;
> And all beyond that Object, there appears
> The long Retinue of a Prosperous Reign,
> A Series of Successful years,
> In orderly Array, a Martial, manly Train.[169]

Dryden was never very lucky in his prophecies; he had foretold that Cromwell's 'bones would rest in a peaceful urn'; his 'long retinue of a prosperous reign' for James II was equally unfortunate.

Philip Ayres, who could be very pretty in a light lyrical manner, over-reached himself in his efforts to praise the new king—

> I paint the prince the world would surely crave
> Could they the sum of all their wishes have....

and after forty lines of adulation concluded with

> At sea his naval power he stretches far
> In Europe holds the scales of peace and war—
> His actions lasting monuments shall frame
> None leave to future age so sweet a name
> Add ten times more, the royal image must
> Fall short of James the Great, the Good, the Just.[170]

Although James II, like Charles I before him, refused to have a coronation procession and thus did many of his good subjects out of a show, the occasion was freely celebrated by the ballad writers, one of them hailing him—

> As if he were on purpose sent
> To fill the English nation with content.[171]

Another ballad writer in lines called *London's Loyalty* comes nearer to the real reason for his subjects' acceptance of him and catches the mood of optimistic resignation, the general desire to avoid further trouble, which had been the cause of the popular reaction in favour of the late king and now of his Roman Catholic brother.

> Honest fellow live content
> Kindly take what God hath sent

> Think what way to pay thy rent
> And strive to fly no higher.
> He's a fool at any rate
> Meddleth with the Church or State
> He'll repent when 'tis too late
> And say that I'm no liar.
> Fear the Lord, Honour the King
> Submit to Fate *in everything*....[172]

'He's a fool at any rate, Meddleth with the Church or State' might be applied to kings as well as to subjects. The weakness of the 'let well alone' school in politics is that everything depends on the government being as willing as the governed to let well alone. Changes from above will inspire mutters from below and this cheerfully negative mood is bound to dissolve rapidly when authority 'meddles with Church or State'.

The accession of a Roman Catholic king was followed by several widely advertised conversions at Court, and the Whig satirists, who had been silent for some time, were encouraged by an easy target. Thus an anonymous writer in a piece called *The Man of No Honour* sums up the arguments of the self-interested:

> Of all philosophies that plagu'd the World,
> And curious Brains in various Labyrinths hurl'd,
> None far'd so ill, and yet so justly far'd,
> As those preached Vertue for its own Reward....

It is better advice to forget about virtue and look for reward. Great are the recompenses which await the time-server:

> You'll soar above, exhal'd by Princely Rays,
> And with Contempt look down on rotten Praise;
> Laugh at dull Notions of a glorious Name,
> When Beggary's the Basis of its Frame....
> Permit no bugbear Thoughts against your Cause,
> The loss of your Religion and the Laws,
> Trifles to those who dare their God defy,
> And can with copious Consciences comply....
> Old Honesty some poor Employ may get,
> But he that sticks at nothing shall be great,
> The Villain wisely thrives in every State.[173]

Among the converts was Dryden, a change of religion which provoked an outburst of derisive comment. He was not allowed to forget that he had once praised Cromwell and a malicious lampoon retailing his life history was circulated:

> What after this could we expect from Thee?
> What could we hope for, but just what we see?
> Scandal to all Religions New and Old;
> Scandal to thine, where Pardon's bought and sold,
> And mortgag'd Happiness redeem'd for Gold.
> Tell me, for 'tis a Truth you must allow;
> Who ever chang'd more in one Moon, than thou?
> Even thine own *Zimri* was more stedfast known;
> He had but one Religion, or had none.
> What Sect of Christians is't thou hast not known,
> And at one time or other made thy own?[174]

The result of Dryden's conversion was that most misconceived of all his political poems *The Hind and the Panther* which appeared in the spring of 1687. In this the Catholic Church is represented by 'a milk white Hind immortal and unchanged' and the Church of England by the Panther 'sure the noblest next the

Hind, the fairest creature of the spotted kind'. Sects are associated with less pleasing beasts. But quite apart from the inherent absurdity of the fable, for nobody can take seriously a panther which 'the crosier wielded and the mitre wore', it suffers also from uncertainty of political aim.

Dryden began it just after his conversion, when King James was relying on the support of the Church of England for his policy of toleration for Roman Catholics; he finished it when it had already become clear that the king aimed not at toleration for Roman Catholics but at their total dominance. The Church of England closed ranks against him and became the chief stumbling-block in his way. Thus Dryden's Panther changes character and becomes steadily less likeable. The reader not only has to accept a fable in which these wild creatures lengthily discuss the doctrine of the Real Presence, or the scandal of the Popish Plot, but is continually baffled by not knowing what Dryden wants him to think of the Panther—if to think at all.

The Hind and the Panther, in spite of occasional graces and the habitual smooth skill of the verse, deserves the mockery of the contemporary satirist who attacked its author because he had

> put a senseless banter
> upon the world with Hind and Panther,
> Making the beasts and birds o' th' wood
> Debate what *he* ne'er understood,

> Deep secrets in Philosophy
> And mysteries in Theology
> All sung in wretched Poetry.[175]

The poetry is, in fact, the only thing about it that is not wretched, though it suffers from the absurdity of the whole design.

In so far as *The Hind and the Panther* puts forward an idea, it is the same idea as that which inspired *Absalom and Achitophel*: belief in tranquil submission to authority. But even in this Dryden cannot be consistent because, if the Hind is to be restored to her rights, there must be a radical change in the spiritual authority accepted in England.

The finest part of the poem is the plea for toleration though this is ungraciously prefaced by an attack on the 'wolfish crew' of sects:

> From *Celtique* Woods is chas'd the *wolfish* Crew
> But ah! some Pity e'en to Brutes is due,
> Their native Walks, methinks, they might enjoy
> Curb'd of their native Malice to destroy.

Then follows the noble plea:

> Of all the Tyrannies on humane kind
> The worst is that which Persecutes the Mind.
> Let us but weigh at what offence we strike,
> 'Tis but because we cannot think alike.
> In punishing of this, we overthrow
> The Laws of Nations and of Nature too.
> Beasts are the Subjects of Tyrannick sway,
> Where still the stronger on the weaker Prey.

Man only of a softer mold is made;
Not for his Fellows ruin, but their Aid.
Created kind, beneficent and free,
The noble Image of the Deity.[176]

This unimpeachable sentiment was probably sincere. Can he have been equally sincere when forty lines further on he asseverates that 'the harmless Hind' was 'never of the persecuting kind'? Passing over Foxe's *Book of Martyrs* and the fires at Smithfield on which so many of Dryden's Protestant compatriots (and very likely he himself) had been reared, Louis XIV had in the year of James's accession revoked the Edict of Nantes, which protected the Huguenots; the Englishmen to whom Dryden addressed this plea for toleration, coupled with the assurance that the Hind, the Roman Catholic Church, was perfectly harmless, were receiving at that very time streams of Protestant refugees from France with hair-raising tales of the persecution from which they had escaped. This was, to say the least of it, unfortunate in relation to King James's plan for restoring a Catholic domination under cover of a policy of general toleration.

While Dryden's Hind and Panther sat discussing theology with folded paws and sheathed claws, an anonymous satirist commented tersely on the army which King James had recently raised. Ostensibly intended to quell the Monmouth rising, the army remained in being after the rising had ended, conveniently encamped on Hounslow Heath.

> Now pause, and view the Army Royal
> Compos'd of valiant Souls and loyal;
> Not rais'd (as ill-Men say) to hurt ye,
> But to defend, or to convert ye:
> For that's the Method now in use,
> The Faith *Tridentine* to diffuse.
> Time was, the Word was powerful;
> But now, tis thought remiss and dull;
> Has not that Energy and Force,
> Which is in well-armed Foot and Horse.[177]

The writer no doubt expected a good number of his readers to hear in this last couplet an echo of *Hudibras*:

> Such as do build their Faith upon
> The holy Text of *Pike* and *Gun*;
> Decide all Controversies by
> Infallible *Artillery*....

a recollection which would link the troops of King James to the military rule of the Puritans and thus achieve a kind of sleight of hand in political argument by driving home a comparison between King James's army, raised for the strengthening of his monarchical authority, with the Army of Saints which had destroyed his father, and whose rule in England had been so bitterly unpopular thirty years before. It was the kind of comparison that would stir uneasy questionings in the heart of many a Royalist.

Poetry, with its easily memorable rhymes, is more suited than prose for conveying concealed hints of this kind to the receptive mind. The satire of this period is full of them, not always immediately recognisable by the modern reader.

The king's attacks on municipal and civil liberties were by now a cause of general alarm, and as his aggressive ineptitude gradually united Churchman and Dissenter, Whig and Tory against him, the greatest flurry and fury of verbal attack, of doggerel and satire, the century had yet witnessed blew up into a storm.

At first there had been too much facile praise of the king. Dryden had been echoed by others less skilful—by Thomas Flatman, by Philip Ayres; even the octogenarian Waller had time to breathe a line about 'our matchless King' before he died in 1687. These verses of hollow praise provoked mocking parodies. It is odd that satire by parody of this kind had not been more general in the earlier part of the century; it is as effective as it is easy, and would seem to be the obvious rejoinder to the lavish over-praise of the typical Court verse of the time:

> Here you may see Great James the Second,
> (The greatest of our Kings he's reckoned!)
> A Hero of such high Renown,
> Whole Nations tremble at his Frown,
> And when he smiles, Men die away
> In Transports of excessive Joy....
> His other Gifts we need but name,
> They are so spread abroad by Fame;
> His Faith, his Zeal, his Constancy,
> Aversion to all Bigotry!

> His firm adhering to the Laws,
> By which he judges every Cause,
> And deals to all impartial Justice,
> In which the Subjects greatest Trust is....
> His governing his brutal Passions
> With far more Rigour than his Nations,
> Would not be sway'd by's Appetite
> Were he to gain an Empire by't.
> From hence does flow that Chastity,
> Temperance, Love, Sincerity,
> And unaffected Piety;
> That just abhorrence of Ambition,
> Idolatry and Superstition,
> Which through his life have shin'd so bright,
> That naught could dazzle their clear Light.[178]

The rhythm is the octosyllabic jog-trot of *Hudibras*, the metre reserved for mockery. Rewritten into heroic couplets, could the same passage be perfectly serious? Philip Ayres's lines:

> Add ten times more, the Royal image must
> Fall short of James, the Great, the Good, the Just.[179]

are scarcely less absurd, but we cannot doubt that his intention was serious, or at least obsequious. The malicious and insulting intention of the octosyllabic rhymester is equally clear, and on examination he seems to rely very largely on the bumping metre to make clear to the reader that he means throughout the exact opposite of what he says.

The same technique of satire by fulsome praise was used, taking Dryden's name in vain, in the *Humble Address of your Majesty's Poet Laureate on the Declaration of Indulgence*—

183

> Great Sir, your healing Declaration
> Has cur'd a base distemper'd Nation....
> 'Tis your peculiar Excellency
> To indulge Religion to a Frensy....

Inspired by the first Declaration of Indulgence, by which King James tried to win the Dissenters to support a policy of toleration designed for the ultimate benefit of Roman Catholics, this satirist detailed the king's attack on the universities and on the corporations, and the revival (with the blessing of some of the judges) of the dispensing power of the Crown. His lines expressed a mock-sycophantic hope,

> That all wou'd sacrifice in course
> Their stubborn Consciences to yours;
> That th' Academies would oppose
> On no Pretence your Royal Cause....
> That Corporations yield their Charters,
> And no more grudge their Soldiers Quarters;
> Your judges too will overawe
> The poor dead Letter of the Law....[180]

After the Revolution of 1688 the ballad writers would amuse themselves over the subservience of the judges, reserving their virulence for Jefferies, their scorn for lesser men like Sir Thomas Jenner who, though he supported the dispensing power of the Crown, had opposed the king in other matters. Ballad writers were not strict for accuracy: they made him say:

> By Great *James* I was raised to the Common-Pleas Bench,
> 'Cause he saw I had exquisite Politick Sense,

184

Which his Wisdom perceived in the Future Tense;
This it is to be learned and witty.

He had my Opinion, that 'twas in his Power
To destroy all the Laws in less than an hour,
For which I may chance to be sent to the Tower;
This it is to be learned and witty.[181]

But this outspokenness of the ballads was for a later
time. In the two years preceding the Revolution, as
before in the 1630's, they amused the public with
horrid murders, and left outspoken political comment to more sophisticated hands whose work was
passed round coffee-houses and scattered in the
streets.

In their work we can trace the growing unity
between Tory and Whig when it became clear that
the endangered Church was in fact prepared to stand
firm against the king's attack. Thus at first the
Dissenters (to judge by satirists in sympathy with
them) were not impressed by the objections raised
by the Church to the first Declaration of Indulgence
in 1687—and suspected that the clergy's increasing
opposition to the king reflected nothing but their
dismay at his invasion of their rights and posses-
sions. They would have been more than human if
they had not felt a certain *Schadenfreude* at the discomfiture of the Anglican prelates who had, after all,
acquiesced in the accession of a Roman Catholic
king and themselves put the Crown on his head.
So, shortly after the first Declaration of Indulgence

comes this cynical mock dialogue between an Anglican and a Catholic priest. The Anglican protests at the king's policy:

> And can our boasted loyalty return
> No other payment but contempt and scorn?
> And must a transsubstantiating priest
> Be with our goodly lands and lordships blest?
> Nay did we all for this the Church disown
> And coin a new religion of our own?
> Of a more spruce and fashionable make
> Than was the old, and boldly undertake
> By scripture for to prove the *Common Prayer*
> When we well know there's no such matter there?...
> And whoso'ere the business would dispute
> We did by fines and pillory confute.
> O precious book, the dearest thing that's ours,
> Except our livings and our *sine cures*.

To this the Roman Catholic priest replies:

> Twas rancour, envy, mere revenge and spite
> That made ye thus against fanatics fight
> And the dear dread of losing all ye had
> That first engaged your malice on our side,

but concludes by promising not to forget his services, whereat the mollified Anglican is contented—

> For when I thought my livelihood was gone
> It was no wonder that I so took on,
> Therefore, dear Sir, let us our hearts combine
> And both in league against Dissenters join.[182]

This embittered attitude to the Anglican hierarchy broke down when the second Declaration of Indulgence in 1688 made it clear to the Dissenters that they were being used as a stalking-horse for the Catholics, and the protest of the Seven Bishops suddenly made the Church the principal bulwark of liberty and Protestantism.

> True *Englishmen*, drink a good Health to the *Mitre*,
> Let our Church ever flourish tho' her Enemies spite her:
> May their Cunning and Forces no longer prevail,
> And their Malice, as well as their Arguments, fail.
> Then remember the Seven which supported our Cause
> As stout as our Martyrs, and as just as our Laws.[183]

This kind of enthusiastic ballad comment is strikingly at variance with the popular comments on bishops earlier in the century, when ballad writers had joyfully recorded in 1641:

> They went to the Tower as the old year ended
> By a dozen together in frosty weather—

The whirligig of time had certainly brought in its revenges with a king inept and ill-advised enough to force the Church on which the first Stuarts had counted as a bulwark to the throne, to become identified with the opposite cause.

A fortnight before the trial and acquittal of the Seven Bishops King James's wife gave birth to a son, on Trinity Sunday, 10 June 1688. Until that moment the ageing king had seemed an endurable evil, because his heir was his Protestant daughter, the Princess of Orange. Dryden was not altogether happily inspired when he made Whitsunday and Trinity Sunday play their part in his congratulatory

poem, *Britannia Rediviva*, which was published within
ten days of the auspicious occasion.

> Last solemn Sabbath saw the Church attend,
> The Paraclete in fiery Pomp descend:
> But when his wondrous Octave rowl'd again
> He brought a Royal Infant in his Train,
> So great a Blessing to so good a King
> None but th' Eternal Comforter cou'd bring.[184]

In view of the general astonishment at the birth of
the child the reference to the Holy Ghost was unfortunate, and was very quickly picked up to add a
spice of blasphemy to the stories that immediately
circulated about the infant Prince of Wales, politically speaking one of the most unpopular babies
ever born. That he was not the king's was widely
believed, and this version got quickly into the
broader of the lampoons. One of these represents
the queen's dead mother, the Duchess of Modena,
intervening from on high:

> When to Heaven she came (for thither she went)
> Each Angel received her with Joy and Content.
> On her knees she fell down before the bright Throne
> And beg'd that God's Mother would grant her one Boon;
> Give England a son (at this Critical Point)
> To put little *Orange*'s Nose out of Joint.[185]

She gets her wish, and a few verses later her
daughter, Mary of Modena, is represented urging
James not to worry about an heir but to leave it all
to her, and to ask no questions about the cause of
her pregnancy. The more generally accepted story

was that the child was not the queen's either, but a supposititious baby introduced by the connivance of the midwife—and not very efficiently at that:

This bantling was heard at St James's to squall
Which made the Queen make so much haste from Whitehall.[186]

Less than three weeks after the child's birth had wrecked the hope of Protestant succession, the secret invitation went out to William of Orange who landed in the autumn, while the ballad-makers of London, safe with a vocal majority behind them, were circulating in different variations *The Song of the Orange*:

> Good People, come by
> The Fruit that I cry,
> That now is in Season, tho' winter is nigh;
> 'Twill do you all good,
> And sweeten your Blood,
> I'm sure it will please you when once understood,
> 'Tis an Orange.[187]

The king's sparse supporters tried to come back with another version: 'Good people I pray, throw the Orange away'—but without much effect.

By far the most influential song of the Revolution was *Lilliburlero* whose author, Lord Wharton, claimed that he had sung James II out of three kingdoms. 'Sung' is the operative word. The doggerel verses are only interesting because they exploit a constantly recurrent theme of the century, the conviction (not by any means baseless) that the king intended to master his recalcitrant English Protestant subjects with the help of his Catholic Irish ones. This suspicion had been the match which set the Civil War alight and lost Charles I his throne. It was almost equally important in firing the mine under James II, and indeed if we throw the song of *Lilliburlero* in among the imponderables of history it was probably more important. The words are a mock dialogue in which two Irishmen, in badly imitated brogue, discuss the imminent throat-cutting of all the English. What mattered was not the words, but the tune from Purcell to which they were set, and the tune was one of those which was liable to win a war, or a cause, or an election for any party lucky enough and astute enough to make it their own. But my subject is the written or spoken word, and not the deeper, less explicit appeal of music, so I can pursue that question no further.

The Revolution of 1688 is the limit of this excursion through the political verse of the century. It is true that the richest and some of the most famous satires of the century lie on the further side of the boundary, after the censorship of the press had lapsed in 1695, but the satire of that last decade and of the opening years of the eighteenth century is a study in itself on which I cannot now embark. I would like instead to look back over the ground traversed and pick up one or two elusive threads of argument.

When I first began to think about this subject I had intended to confine myself, if not always to poetry in the highest sense, at least to verse written by those with some claim to rank as poets. But as the material accumulated I felt that the inclusion of popular ballads was essential to the argument.

In spite of the great gulf which divides spontaneous popular doggerel from the polished productions of the study there was, during this epoch of general political disturbance, constant reaction between the two. This was at its most noticeable during the Civil War, when a poet of the sophistication of John Denham simply made over and parodied the naïve exaggerations of the folk ballad in a skit like *The Western Wonder*. This is particularly interesting because Denham, in his character as poet rather than propagandist, was a self-conscious and sophisticated artist, a pioneer of the rhymed couplet and a forerunner in creating the well-mannered, unexaggerated descriptive landscape verse which became popular in the eighteenth century. In the same year in which his lively and rollicking *Western Wonder* became a popular song, he published for connoisseurs his careful, pretty and boring *Cooper's Hill* with its famous lines on the Thames:

> O could I flow like thee, and make thy stream
> My great example, as it is my theme!
> Though deep, yet clear, though gentle, yet not dull,
> Strong without rage, without o'er-flowing full.[188]

Occasionally the opposite happened and the ballad writer picked up and adapted phrases from a more elegant world. So the 'Ask me no more' device of polite lyrics, best known in Thomas Carew's 'Ask me no more where Jove bestows, When June is past, the fading rose', was adapted to serve the political ballad:

> Aske me no more, why there appears
> Dayly such troops of Dragoneers,
> Since it was requisite, you know,
> They rob, *cum privilegio.*[189]

There is thus a temporary alliance, or at least a flowing together, a coalescence between sophisticated and unsophisticated verse at the time of the Civil War and the Commonwealth, especially among the Cavaliers. The development began naturally enough with the attempts of the king's supporters to catch the ear of a wider audience; it was strengthened when with the defeat of the Cavaliers the drinking song or ballad became one of the few remaining, and relatively safe, ways of expressing pent-up feelings. So grew up that lightly satirical popular verse always facile, often witty, of which Alexander Brome was the principal exponent.

This joining up of the two streams, the popular and the sophisticated, did not last for long. It is not altogether accidental that it should occur during the Civil War and the years immediately succeeding, when the rigid hierarchic social structure had been badly jarred by the war and the opinions, both religious and political, of ordinary men were for the first time being freely and widely expressed.

After 1660 satire became the obvious weapon for the armoury of the opposition, trying to reassemble their forces against an overwhelming popular reaction in favour of king and Court, and working under the difficulties imposed by a fierce censorship. Satire is essentially a sophisticated weapon, demanding in the reader a readiness to catch and understand allusions, and an appreciation of the ironic, the exaggerated and the oblique. The work of Marvell and his imitators aimed at an educated and informed public. So too did Dryden and the Tory satirists who followed him.

Meanwhile street-ballad commentary, divorced from instructed comment and pursuing its own course, dropped to a very low level of banality. The demand for the ballad was still there, and the number of them did not decline; the easy doggerel comments on coronation, royal wedding, sea-battle or political plot held their own with tales of love, murder and strange apparitions, but the quality of the comment became thin and uninteresting; trivial platitudes were strung together with the barest attention to rhyme or metre. There was little in the later years of the century to compare with the zest and swinging, spontaneous ease of, for instance, Martin Parker's ballads in its earlier years. With the exception of one or two more lively effusions called forth by the events of 1688 the general level of popular balladry, as the century proceeds, is depressingly flat.

These later ballads have, however, some interesting characteristics. They contain, for instance, an increasing number of references to economic conditions. From time to time, to be sure, money or the lack of it had played a part in popular verses earlier in the century. But by the last quarter of the century it had a way of getting in everywhere. One ballad linked the Popish Plot to a trade depression and accused the Papists of destroying London's trade. Again that 'let well alone' ballad which I quoted on the coronation of James II brings in, as a prime preoccupation of the ordinary citizen, the paying of his rent. This is no doubt very true to life, but rent-paying is, all the same, an odd intruder in a ballad on a coronation. In the 1680's 'The Poor Folks' Complaint', or 'The Hardness of the Times' were frequent ballad subjects, and few political events were celebrated in doggerel without some reference to the state of trade.

Generalisations are dangerous, but this tendency in the popular ballads evidently reflected the ruling passions and interests of their buyers and readers; anti-Popery, their other ruling passion, became ever more closely bound up with the theme of economic interest. This was not new in itself. As early as 1625

Martin Parker had revealed the connection in *Let us to the Wars again*—

> France and Flanders make no moan
> They get riches we get none....
> But *true religion* to maintain
> Let us to the wars again.

That enshrines the cheerfully arrogant idea that a war for religion and the Protestant cause—sincere of course—will pay dividends. The note sixty years later had become more querulous and defensive. The continuous machinations of Popish neighbours against English trade were frequently hinted at: the foundations of the 'Popery and Wooden Shoes' obsession of a later period were being firmly laid.

Up to the Civil War the ballads, when they dealt with politics, on the whole reflected, if in rather cruder form, the prejudices and ideas of the average educated man. The anti-Spanish demonstrations of the populace in the reign of King James I were the noisier counterpart of speeches made by the opponents of the Crown inside the House of Commons. Cheerfully aggressive ballads reflected this feeling in simpler terms, but with much the same fervour as the elaborate verses of poets like Phineas Fletcher. Because sophisticated and unsophisticated versification drew on a common stock of political prejudices, it was possible to exploit the ballad effectively in the Civil War; this was done by the Cavaliers in their gay parodies, or, rather more rarely, in a stirring call to arms for the Parliamentary cause.

By the end of the century the sophisticated and the unsophisticated, once so closely linked, had moved very far away from each other. The ballads had become the vehicles of ideas altogether thinner and cruder than those dealt with in satire. There was here, as in almost every other branch of culture, a division of taste, a separation which was ultimately to become a gulf between popular and educated forms of expression.

This is a large and controversial problem which has been treated as it affects drama or poetry by many historians of literature. But it is interesting to see that the division occurs clearly even in the field of political comment, which from its very nature has to draw its inspiration from actual happenings and experiences which are, in one form or another, common to a whole society.

The most usual kind of political verse—that is, verse devoted to a political subject—is in this century still the complimentary poem addressed to monarch or statesman on a ceremonial occasion or in honour of some event. In general it is just these parts of a poet's work that receive least attention because of their ephemeral or conventional character. With a lesser poet such selection is easy enough; the sycophantic excesses of Waller and Davenant, who changed sides and uttered praise first of one side and then of another, are not very noticeable in the perspective of time; we do not remember them for their political poems anyway. But a great poet, like Dryden, must pay the penalty of greatness. We cannot fail to know his political record or to take notice of the poems which mark out his shifting opinions.

> O gracious God! How far have we
> Prophan'd thy Heav'nly Gift of Poesy!
> Made prostitute and profligate the Muse,
> Debas'd to each obscene and impious use,
> Whose Harmony was first ordain'd above
> For tongues of *Angels*, and for *Hymns* of *Love*![190]

These famous lines of repentance, in the *Ode to the pious memory of Anne Killigrew* written in 1686, refer of course to the way in which, in his plays, he had yielded to the corrupt taste of his 'lubric and adulterate' age. They might equally refer to the too frequent and too easy praise that he had poured out on distinguished personages whom he wished to please.

Yet it is probable that he himself felt no particular regret for any of these lines of adulation except those he had written on Cromwell in youth. He was essentially a conventional man, and this kind of poem was, after all, in the accepted convention of his time. For us, it is not so easy a convention to accept, especially in literature. We can adapt ourselves more willingly to it in other arts. Titian's great 'Gloria' in the Prado shows the entire family of the Emperor Charles V rapt in the heights of heaven adoring the Trinity, though several of them were still on earth when the picture was painted; but Titian is not generally criticised as a syco-phantic painter on this account. Nor do we think poorly of Rubens for his 'Apotheosis of James I'. It could be argued that Titian and Rubens were craftsmen commissioned to paint certain subjects and that they merely fulfilled their contracts; whereas the poets who arranged for throngs of angels to escort King James VI into England, who fixed Charles I in the sky as a constellation, who praised the justice of Charles II and the equanimity of James II, were acting spontaneously and in hopes of royal favour. But is there very much difference except that Titian and Rubens were fairly sure of their payment, whereas for the poets reward was, at best, very uncertain?

It still remains something of a mystery that the painter's lavish praise is more easily acceptable to us: an extravagance that we know and take for what it is, while the equivalent in words is much harder to accept. I doubt if any of us here would rock with laughter at the contemplation of the Rubens ceiling at Whitehall. It is a great work of art and we take it as such. Carew's masque, glorifying the Stuart monarchy in much the same way, provokes a smile. No doubt Thomas Carew was only a minor artist in words, whereas Rubens was a major artist in colour and form, so that the comparison is in that case rather out of scale. But we do not usually laugh at the courtly and flattering work of painters much inferior to Rubens—that of Thornhill at Greenwich for instance, or Lebrun at Versailles. The appeal is, after all, to the eye, and the eye will accept things at a sensual level without moral judgment. The poet aims more immediately at the intellect, and must take the consequences.

Yet luxuriant praise in verse, when it is really beautiful, should be acceptable however incongruous or unworthy the subject. Under an expert hand the convention flowers into beauty:

> But who can always on the billows lie?
> The watery wilderness yields no supply.
> Spreading our sails to Harwich we resort,
> And meet the Beauties of the British Court.
> The illustrious Duchess and her glorious train,
> (Like Thetis with her nymphs) adorn the main,
> The gazing sea-gods, since the Paphian Queen
> Sprung from among them, no such sight had seen.
> Charmed with the graces of a troop so fair,
> Those deathless powers for us themselves declare,
> Resolved the aid of Neptune's Court to bring,
> And help the nation where such beauties spring;
> The soldier here his wanted store supplies
> And takes new valour from the ladies' eyes.[191]

That is Edmund Waller, whose behaviour has come in for a good deal of criticism in these pages. The context was a bloody and hard fought naval war;

seamen were unpaid and their families in want while the illustrious Duchess—stout, self-indulgent, and of somewhat smirched reputation—visited her husband the royal Admiral at Harwich. This incongruity and heartlessness called forth savage parody, and met its reward in those virulent satires of the 'Instructions to a Painter' series. But in themselves, and out of context, Waller's lines have an elegant enchantment.

Dryden on such a theme of compliment could scarcely fail; his welcome to another Duchess on her return from Scotland I have already cited. Here he is on a third Duchess—Ormonde this time—on her return to Ireland—

> At Your Approach, they crowded to the Port;
> And scarcely Landed, You create a Court:
> As *Ormond's* Harbinger, to You they run,
> For Venus is the promise of the Sun.
> The Waste of Civil Wars, their Towns destroy'd,
> *Pales* unhonoured, Ceres unemploy'd,
> Were all forgot; and one Triumphant Day
> Wip'd all the Tears of these Campaigns away.
> Blood, Rapines, Massacres, were cheaply bought,
> So mighty Recompense Your Beauty brought.
> As when the Dove returning bore the Mark
> Of Earth restor'd to the long-lab'ring Ark,
> The Relicks of Mankind, secure of Rest,
> Op'd every Window to receive the Guest,
> And the fair Bearer of the Message bless'd;
> So, when You came, with loud repeated Cries,
> The Nation took an Omen from your Eyes,
> And God advanc'd his Rainbow in the Skies.[192]

Out of their political context, they are lines of flawless grace. In the context of the bloodthirsty and intolerant Anglo-Irish struggle of the mid-seventeenth century, they ring hollow. How happy for the future relations of Ireland and England it would have been if the Duchess of Ormonde's beauty could indeed have wiped the tears of three campaigns away.

It is not wise, it is probably not fair, to think about the political context of such ecstatic lines of praise. What does very clearly emerge from the study of this kind of verse is that only a superlative artist can succeed in it. When Shadwell gets going on the return of Queen Mary II, the result is threadbare and pretentious:

> Our adored *Princess*, to *Batavians* lent
> Is home to us with mighty Intrest sent:
> For we, with her, have won the Great *Nassau*,
> Whose Sword shall keep the Papal world in awe.
> She comes, she comes, the Fair, the Good, the Wise,
> With loudest Acclamations rend the Skies;
> Rock all the Steeples, kindle every Street,
> Thunder ye Cannons from each Fort and Fleet....
> Where'er so many sacred Vertues join
> They to a Scepter show a Right Divine....
> For Princes more of solid Glory gain,
> Who are thought fit, than who are born to reign.[193]

Such thumping lack of inspiration serves only to recall those famous lines which Dryden put into the mouth of the dying Flecknoe, bequeathing to Shadwell his supremacy over the realms of nonsense:

> Shadwell alone my perfect image bears,
> Mature in dullness from his tender years;
> Shadwell alone of all my Sons is he
> Who stands confirm'd in full stupidity.
> The rest to some faint meaning make pretence,
> But Shadwell never deviates into sense.
> Some Beams of Wit on other souls may fall,
> Strike through and wake a lucid intervall;
> But Shadwell's genuine night admits no ray,
> His rising Fogs prevail upon the Day.... [194]

Dryden is not fair in saying that Shadwell 'never deviates into sense'. The lines in his poem on Queen Mary, which suggest that merit makes a nobler claim to sovereignty than birth, are much better sense than Dryden's views on the Duchesses of York or Ormonde, let alone the opinions uttered by Carew, Cartwright and others on the divinity of James I, Charles I, their wives and progeny. The fault of Shadwell is that he never (or rarely) deviates into poetry, a fault which cannot be fastened on the soaring adulations of Waller, Dryden and the others. Does this suggest that meaning and context even in political verse is not so very important after all? That what ultimately matters is the imagery and the music?

Perhaps Shadwell, the obvious butt and booby, had better be left out of the argument. In no circumstances, and with no subject, would he have been even a passable poet. (He was a lively and efficient writer of comedies: his talent was essentially earthy, colloquial and prosaic.) But if we consider only those, among writers of complimentary verse, who had authentic gifts, and particularly the early Caroline group—Carew, Cartwright, Townshend, Lovelace, Cowley—and compare them with the later poets, Dryden and the mature Waller, something about the importance of meaning, or at least of feeling, does begin to emerge. The point is a delicate one, and I am aware that there is probably more of the historian than of the literary critic in what I have to say on it.

The Courtly verse of the later epoch, the time of Charles II, has not the vigorous extravagance of that of the earlier period; it lacks the fantastic and often absurd daring. Compare the earlier and the later poems of Edmund Waller. To praise the naval programme of King Charles I he could do no less than call down a second deluge and picture the English fleet triumphant over a submerged world. But when he came to write of the naval victories of Charles II in his poem on the sea-fight of June 1665 for instance, his facile exaggerations sprang from recognisable events. They were prettified but not wholly imaginary. The earlier poets, the writers of the brief halcyon years of King Charles I, appear altogether remote from reality. Thomas Carew fixed Charles I and Henrietta Maria as stars in heaven; and William Cartwright saw the creation of the world from chaos in the espousals of their nine-year-old daughter. At their boldest and best the Court poems of the earlier period have a richness of imagination which ravishes us completely and compels us to suppress the critical promptings of common sense. They do, of course, swing dizzily between the delightful and the ridiculous: their imagination plunges without restraint towards regions where the flight cannot possibly be sustained and they must crash in disastrous absurdity. Poets outbid each other in the extravagance of their praise and there seemed to be no accepted frontiers to bound their claims for the virtues and powers of royalty.

By the time of Charles II the convention was established and had its own rules; but it was by then a modified convention, essentially decorative; and poets worked to its rules not aiming—as their predecessors had done—to strike at some dazzling truth at the heart of all this exaggeration. Is that the key? Were the earlier poets, flattery apart, still hoping for some revelation? They truly believed in Divine Right and their attitude to the king had something of the fervour and intensity of their attitude to God. King Charles I had believed himself with deep sincerity to be God's vice-gerent; to that extent the poetic compliments which placed him among the stars and bestowed cosmic significance on the births, deaths and marriages in his family were related to political ideas seriously and passionately held. King Charles II had every practical intention of maintaining and increasing his monarchical power by any convenient theory or practice, but he was too much of a realist and of a sensualist to hold any sustained conviction of his own near-divinity. The Court poetry of his reign pleased therefore by its technical skill, by the prettiness of its sound, by the charm with which it filled out the accepted conventions of praise; the ideas are commonplace and they are not meant to be taken seriously.

Early Caroline poetry, on the other hand, is meant to be taken seriously. Here is one more example from Carew, the most extravagant of them all. It is an allusion to the masque, *Tempe Restor'd*, written for Queen Henrietta Maria by Townshend in 1633. The queen's singing is the subject of the lines:

> But when the Queene of Beautie did inspire
> The ayre with perfumes, and our hearts with fire,
> Breathing from her celestiall Organ sweet
> Harmonious notes, our soules fell at her feet,
> And did with humble reverend dutie, more
> Her rare perfections, than high state adore.[195]

Carew is using the queen as a symbol of the yearning towards perfection of all mortal things. He means it, as much as any lover might mean it when writing of his mistress. We are willing to accept in poetry the transfiguring effects of love; there is no reason why we should not also accept the transfiguring effects of political beliefs. The reason that we do not do so, is that we suspect the poet of an interested motive when he praises a king or queen, a motive which is absent when he praises his mistress. Of course, the selfish motive is there: Carew wished to please the queen because of his place as a courtier and hers as a dispenser of patronage. He wished to please her just as Waller and Dryden wished to please the Duchesses of York and Ormonde, or King Charles II. But the desire to please is not the only or even the most important element that inspired the poem: we do Carew and his contemporaries a grave injustice if we think so. There was also a desire to contemplate and to write about the mystical qualities of royalty in much the same spirit as they contemplated and wrote about beauty or holiness.

Between the two epochs comes the Protectorate of Cromwell. Marvell, who most eloquently celebrated its glories, achieved in his praise of the Protector a more convincing and better balanced comment than is usual in the Court or State verse either of the earlier or later time. He was fortunate in his subject; indeed he was not the man to write verse of this kind without a subject fit to inspire him. The greatness of Cromwell, a man who rose by natural merit, was a theme that suited peculiarly well Marvell's views on the part played by God and nature, by matter and spirit, in the harmony of the universe. He is the only poet of the century who can make political verse fit into a balanced view of life. He is nearer to the early Caroline poets, his predecessors, in seeking for truth and meaning in the contemplation of the Head of the State, more fortunate in being able, to his own satisfaction, to find it. He is remote from the empty triviality of the later epoch; indeed the bitterness with which he satirised Waller may have been not only the bitterness of the angry Puritan and political opponent, but the deeper bitterness of a poet who sees the art which he loves debased to unworthy uses.

The time of the first four Stuarts witnessed a profound change in outlook. Fanatical religious faith gave way to indifference. The age of reason was approaching by the end of the century, a change usually ascribed to the increasing study of the natural sciences although the connection between the two things is not always so clear as it can be made to appear. The old hierarchy of society had been gradually transformed, and the era of commercial and industrial expansion had altered the face of England.

The ballads and the satires bring out the harsher aspects of the change. The ballads become duller, more prosaic, lacking in gaiety, as though the springs of natural poetry were drying up with the increasing sophistication of the people. The satires on the other hand, smart, sophisticated, holding nothing sacred, growing a little too facile, reveal a decline of idealism. Belief in Divine Right had collapsed, failing to survive two successive sovereigns who could not morally sustain it; politics had ceased to be a branch of theology, and become a matter of good business judgment, of self-interest and national interest.

To all this the Court poetry added an accompaniment—catching in the time of Charles I, in spite of exaggerations, the authentic note of fervent, even religious, aspiration, declining ultimately into a mere social amenity, a decorative exercise, practised in the margin of Courts that had no noble aspirations at all.

NOTES AND REFERENCES

1   *Poems of Richard Lovelace*, ed. C. H. Wilkinson (Oxford, 1930), p. 81.
2   *The Non-Dramatic Works of Thomas Dekker*, ed. Grosart (London, 1884), vol. I, pp. 97–8.
3   *The Poems of John Donne*, ed. Sir Herbert Grierson (Oxford, 1951), p. 144 (Satyre IIII, lines 101–7, 121–6).
4   *Non-Dramatic Works of Dekker*, vol. I, p. 99.
5   *Ben Jonson*, ed. Herford and Simpon (Oxford 1947), vol. VIII, p. 28.
6   *The Complete Works of Samuel Daniel*, ed. Grosart (London, 1885), vol. I, pp. 143–4.
7   *The Poetical Works of Sir William Alexander*, ed. L. E. Kastner and H. B. Charlton (Manchester, 1929), vol. II, p. 390.
8   *The Poetical Works of Alexander Craig*, ed. David Laing (Hunterian Club, Glasgow, 1873), Part I, pp. 7–8.
9   *Poetical Works of Craig*, Part VII, pp. 5–7.
10 *The Poetical Remains of William Lithgow* (Edinburgh, 1863), 'Scotland's Welcome to her Native Sonne and Soveraigne Lord, King Charles'.
11 *The Poems of Richard Crashaw*, ed. L. C. Martin (Oxford, 1927), pp. 136–7.
12 *The Poetical Works of Giles and Phineas Fletcher*, ed. F. S. Boas (Cambridge, 1900), vol. I, pp. 171–3.
13 *Poetical Works of Alexander*, vol. II, p. 388.
14 *Ben Jonson*, ed. Herford and Simpson, vol. VIII, p. 433.
15 *The Poetical Works of William Drummond of Hawthornden*, ed. L. E. Kastner (Manchester, 1913), vol. I, p. 76.
16 *Non-Dramatic Works of Dekker*, vol. III, pp. 15–16.
17 *The Pepys Ballads*, ed. Hyder E. Rollins (Cambridge, Mass., 1929), vol. I, p. 223.

Notes and References

18 Middleton, *A Game at Chess*, Act v, scene 3.

19 *King James VI and I, Political Works*, ed. McIlwain, *The True Law of Free Monarchies*.

20 *The Poems of Thomas Carew*, ed. Rhodes Dunlap (Oxford, 1949), pp. 35–6.

21 *Poetical Works of Giles and Phineas Fletcher*, vol. 1, pp. 185–6.

22 *Poems and Letters of Andrew Marvell*, ed. H. M. Margoliouth, second edition (Oxford, 1952), vol. 1, p. 69.

23 *Abraham Cowley, Essays, Plays and Verses*, ed. A. R. Waller (Cambridge, 1906), pp. 343–4.

24 *A Pepysian Garland*, ed. Hyder E. Rollins (Cambridge, 1922), pp. 418–19.

25 *Poetical Works of Drummond*, vol. 11, p. 245.

26 *Pepysian Garland*, p. 280.

27 *Poems of Carew*, p. 57.

28 *The Poems of James Shirley*, ed. R. L. Armstrong (New York, 1941), p. 15.

29 *Poems and Songs relating to the Duke of Buckingham*, ed. F. W. Fairholt (Percy Society, London, 1850), pp. 51–2.

30 Fanshawe's poems are included in the 1647 edition of his translation of Guarini, *Il Pastor Fido*.

31 *Ben Jonson*, ed. Herford and Simpson, vol. VIII, p. 430.

32 Aurelian Townshend's *Poems and Masks*, ed. E. K. Chambers (Oxford, 1912), pp. 75, 77.

33 *Ibid.* pp. 79 ff.

34 This poem, not included in Chambers' edition of Townshend, is to be found in Dunlap's edition of *The Poems of Thomas Carew*, Appendix, p. 207.

35 *Poems of Carew*, pp. 75–7.

36 *Ben Jonson*, ed. Herford and Simpson, vol. VIII, pp. 236–7.

37 James Shirley, *Dramatic Works*, ed. Gifford and Dyce (London, 1833), vol. VI, p. 277.

38 *Poems of Carew*, pp. 154–5, 176 (*Coelum Britannicum*, ll. 46–51, 62–70, 90–7, 862–4).

39 *The Poems of Thomas Pestell*, ed. Hannah Buchan (Oxford, 1940), pp. 40, 41, 43.

40   T. Haywood, *True description of his majesties royal ship* (London, 1637).

41   *The Poems of Edmund Waller*, ed. G. Thorn Drury (London, 1905), vol. i, p. 15.

42   *Works of John Suckling*, ed. A. H. Thompson (London, 1910), p. 19.

43   Abraham Cowley, *Poems*, ed. Waller (Cambridge, 1905), pp. 22–4.

44   *A Pepysian Garland*, ed. Hyder E. Rollins (Cambridge, 1922), pp. 456–9.

45   William Davenant, *Salmacida Spolia* (London, 1639/40).

46   *Poems of Crashaw*, pp. 178–9 nn.

47   *Cavalier and Puritan: Ballads and Broadsides illustrating the Great Rebellion*, ed. Hyder E. Rollins (New York, 1923), pp. 78, 82.

48   *Ibid.* p. 85.

49   *Ballads and other Fugitive Poetical Pieces chiefly Scottish, from the collection of Sir James Balfour, Knight*, ed. James Maidment (Edinburgh, 1834), p. 22.

50   William Davenant, *Works* (London, 1673), p. 304.

51   *Scottish Ballads and Songs*, ed. James Maidment (Edinburgh, 1868), vol. i, pp. 339–41.

52   *Cavalier and Puritan*, p. 140.

53   *The Poetical Works of Sir John Denham*, ed. Theodore Howard Banks, Jr. (Yale and Oxford, 1928), pp. 153–4.

54   Guarini, *Il Pastor Fido*, translated by R. Fanshawe (London, 1647), p. 298.

55   G. Saintsbury, *Minor Poets of the Caroline Period* (Oxford, 1905–21), vol. iii, pp. 67–8.

56   *Plays and Poems of William Cartwright*, ed. G. B. Evans (Madison, 1951), pp. 539–40.

57   *Cavalier and Puritan*, p. 127.

58   *Ibid.* pp. 134–5, 138.

59   *Works of John Taylor*, ed. Spenser Society Fourth Collection, Manchester, 1877. No. 12, p. 5.

60   Davenant, *Works*, p. 304.

61 Wither, *The Great Assizes Holden in Parnassus* (London, 1643).

62 *Aubrey's Brief Lives*, ed. Anthony Powell (London, 1949), p. 295.

63 Calendar of State Papers, Domestic, 1644.

64 Saintsbury, *Minor Poets*, vol. III, p. 54.

65 *Works of Henry Vaughan*, ed. L. C. Martin (Oxford, 1957), p. 626.

66 *Works of Robert Herrick*, ed. L. C. Martin (second edition, Oxford, 1956), p. 25.

67 Cowley, *Essays, Plays and Verses*, p. 479.

68 *Poems of William Cartwright*, p. 554.

69 *Musarum Oxoniensium Epibateria* (Oxford, 1643).

70 Saintsbury, *Minor Poets*, vol. III, pp. 66–7.

71 *Poems of William Cartwright*, pp. 556–7.

72 *MS. Memoirs of Richard Augustine Hay* (National Library of Scotland).

73 *Elegies on the death of Colonell John Hampden* (London, 1643).

74 Cowley, *Essays, Plays and Verses*, p. 476.

75 *Ibid.* pp. 151–2.

76 Alexander Brome, *Songs and Poems* (London, 1668), pp. 149–50.

77 *Rump Songs* (1662), vol. I, pp. 11–12.

78 *Ibid.* p. 134; a slightly different version is in the *Poetical Works of Denham*, pp. 130–1.

79 *Aubrey's Brief Lives*, p. 83.

80 Wither, *Campo-Musae* (1643).

81 *Aubrey's Brief Lives*, p. 67.

82 Wither, *Opobalsamum Anglicanum* (1646).

83 *Rump Songs*, vol. I, p. 292; several broadsheet versions with slight variations.

84 *Rump Songs*, vol. I, p. 333; also several broadsheet versions.

85 Brome, *Songs and Poems*, p. 73.

86 *Mercurius Britanicus his Welcome to Hell* (London, 1646), p. 8.

87 Nedham, *A Short History of the English Rebellion compiled in Verse* (London, 1680), p. 9.

88 *Ibid.* pp. 3–4; these verses appeared first week by week in 1647–8 in Nedham's paper *Mercurius Pragmaticus*.

89 Nedham, *Digitus Dei* (London, 1649).

90 *Poems of Montrose*, ed. J. L. Weir (London, 1938), p. 33.

91 Saintsbury, *Minor Poets*, vol. III, pp. 93–4.

92 *Ibid.* pp. 265–6.

93 *Poems and Letters of Marvell*, vol. I, p. 89.

94 Cowley, *Essays, Plays and Verses*, pp. 345, 353.

95 *Cavalier and Puritan*, pp. 238, 248, 252–3.

96 *Ibid.* pp. 316–17.

97 *Wit and Drollery*, by Sir J. M. Ja. S. Sir W. D. J. D. and other admirable Wits. (London, 1656), p. 12; Brome, *Songs and Poems*, p. 50.

98 *Ibid.* p. 87.

99 *Ibid.* pp. 85–7.

100 *Musarum Deliciae or The Muses Recreation*, by Sir John Mennis and James Smith, second edition (London, 1656), p. 10.

101 Brome, *Songs and Poems*, p. 238.

102 *Milton's Poetical Works*, ed. H. C. Beeching (Oxford, 1925), p. 87.

103 Brome, *Songs and Poems*, p. 29; see also *Rump Songs*, vol. I, p. 298.

104 *Rump Songs*, vol. I, p. 317.

105 Wither, *Carmen Eucharisticon* (London, 1649). These verses are taken from a much longer poem; I have reversed the order of the last two as this makes a stronger climax and I cannot feel that the text of Wither is inviolable.

106 *Letters and Poems of Marvell*, vol. I, pp. 111–12.

107 *Ibid.* p. 110.

108 *Poems of Waller*, vol. II, p. 17.

109 *Ibid.* vol. II, pp. 10–11, 17.

110 *Cavalier and Puritan*, p. 345.

111 *Milton's Poetical Works*, ed. H. C. Beeching (Oxford, 1925), p. 84.

112 *Letters and Poems of Marvell*, vol. I, p. 129.

113 *Poems of Waller*, vol. II, pp. 34–5.

114 Wither, *Salt upon Salt* (London, 1659), p. 9.

115 *Poems of John Dryden*, ed. James Kinsley (Oxford, 1958), vol. I, p. 12.

116 Brome, *Songs and Poems*, pp. 197–8.

117 John Collop, *Itur Satyricum* (London, 1660).

118 *Poems of Dryden*, vol. I, p. 20 ('Astraea Redux', ll. 157–78).

119 *Poems of Waller*, vol. II, pp. 35–6.

120 'Astraea Redux', ll. 209–14, 274–5.

121 *Poems of John Wilmot, Earl of Rochester*, ed. V. de Sola Pinto, p. 3.

122 Brome, *Songs and Poems*, p. 45.

123 *Merry Drollery, 1661*, ed. J. W. Ebsworth (London, 1875), pp. 53–4.

124 *Diary of Samuel Pepys*, ed. H. B. Wheatley (London, 1949), vol. II, p. 399; vol. III, p. 30.

125 Samuel Butler, *Hudibras*, ed. A. R. Waller (Cambridge, 1905), p. 133.

126 *Ibid.* p. 42.

127 *Ibid.* p. 157.

128 *Ibid.* p. 3.

129 *Ibid.* p. 224.

130 *Ibid.* p. 8.

131 *Ibid.* p. 9.

132 Saintsbury, *Minor Poets*, vol. I, p. 509.

133 *Poems of Dryden*, vol. I, p. 27 ('A Panegyrick on the Coronation', ll. 89–102, 107–10).

134 *Poems of Waller*, vol. II, pp. 42–5.

135 *Poems on Affairs of State* (1716 edition), vol. I, p. 97.

136 *Poems of Dryden*, vol. I, pp. 81–2, 104 ('Annus Mirabilis', verses 163–7, 297–8).

137 *Poems of Waller*, vol. II, pp. 48–9, 53.

138 *Poems of State*, vol. I, p. 29.

139 *Ibid.* p. 33.

of State, vol. I, part ii, pp. 116–17.

. 129.

. 56.

of Dryden, vol. II, p. 476 ('Hind and Panther', 35–8, 239–50).

of State, vol. I, part ii, p. 54.

p. 53–4.

bury, *Minor Poets*, vol. III, p. 320.

of State, vol. I, part ii, pp. 126–7.

ol. III, p. 314.

ol. I, pp. 222, 224.

ol. I, part ii, pp. 137–8.

of Dryden, vol. II, pp. 541–2 ('Britannia Rediviva', -24).

of State, vol. I, part ii, p. 184.

of State, vol. III, p. 268.

ol. III, p. 286.

al *Works of Denham*, p. 77.

Songs, vol. I, p. 68; also broadsheet versions.

of Dryden, vol. I, p. 461.

of Waller, vol. II, p. 179.

of Dryden, vol. IV, p. 1465 ('To Her Grace the less of Ormond', ll. 60–77).

of State, vol. I, part ii, pp. 178–9.

of Dryden, vol. I, p. 265 (MacFlecknoe, ll. 15–24).

of Carew, p. 76.

Notes

140 Letters and Poems of

141 Poems of State, vol.

142 Ibid. III, p. 52

143 Poems of Rochester,

144 Poems of State, vol.

145 Ibid. p. 113.

146 Ibid. pp. 253–4.

147 Poems of Rochester,

148 Poems of State, vol.

149 Letters and Poems of

150 Ibid. pp. 194–5.

151 Poems of Rochester,

152 Pepys Ballads, vol.

153 Poems of State, vol.

154 Poems of Dryden, vo
     pp. 318–26).

155 Poems of Dryden, v

156 Poems of Dryden, v

157 Ibid. vol. 1, pp. 217
     ll. 1–11, 45–56).

158 Ibid. ll. 383–4, 389

159 Ibid. ll. 965–8.

160 Ibid. ll. 383–4, 389

161 Ibid. ll. 529–35.

162 Ibid. ll. 585–8.

163 Ibid. ll. 796, 801–

164 Pepys Ballads, vol.

165 Poems of Dryden,

166 Saintsbury, Minor

167 Poems of Dryden,
     verse 13).

168 Saintsbury, Minor

169 Poems of Dryden,
     verse 18).

170 Saintsbury, Minor

171 Pepys Ballads, vo

172 Ibid. p. 159.

173 Poe

174 Ibi

175 Ibi

176 Poe
     1, ll

177 Poe

178 Ibia

179 Sai

180 Poe

181 Ibia

182 Ibia

183 Ibid

184 Poe.
     ll. 1

185 Poer

186 Poer

187 Ibid

188 Poer

189 Rum

190 Poen

191 Poen

192 Poen
     Dut

193 Poen

194 Poen

195 Poen

INDEX

Index

Index

Index